PUBLIC ADMINISTRATION

IN

MASSACHUSETTS:

THE RELATION OF CENTRAL TO LOCAL ACTIVITY

STUDIES IN HISTORY, ECONOMICS AND PUBLIC LAW

EDITED BY THE FACULTY OF POLITICAL SCIENCE OF
COLUMBIA UNIVERSITY
IN THE CITY OF NEW YORK

Volume VIII]   [Number 4

PUBLIC ADMINISTRATION IN MASSACHUSETTS

THE RELATION OF CENTRAL TO LOCAL ACTIVITY

BY

ROBERT HARVEY WHITTEN

AMS PRESS
NEW YORK

TABLE OF CONTENTS

CHAPTER I

INTRODUCTION

CHAPTER II

PUBLIC SCHOOLS

(v)

CHAPTER III

PUBLIC POOR RELIEF

CHAPTER IV

PENAL INSTITUTIONS

CHAPTER V

PUBLIC HEALTH

CHAPTER IX

GAS AND ELECTRIC LIGHT WORKS

CHAPTER X

THE CIVIL SERVICE COMMISSION

CHAPTER XI

CENTRAL AUDIT, LOCAL RECORDS, STATE HIGHWAYS, AND THE METROPOLITAN DISTRICT

CHAPTER XII

Theory of the Relation of Commonwealth to Municipal Activity

CHAPTER I

INTRODUCTION

PUBLIC administration in Massachusetts may be divided into two great periods; (1) the period of settlement and decentralization, and (2) the period of the elimination of distance and centralization. The first movement began with the settlement of the colony, was at its height during the eighteenth century, and came to an end during the first half of the present century: the second had its beginnings in the first half of the present century and still continues.

1. *Period of Settlement and Decentralization.* The first was a period of expansion: population was spreading over the outlying territory. From 1700 to 1770, one hundred and sixty-eight new towns were incorporated.[1] Within the town a process of decentralization and division was going on. When a settlement was made in an outlying portion of a town, it was set off as a district, a precinct or a parish.[2] After it became fully developed, reproducing in itself the conditions of the parent society, maintaining its own school and meeting house, it was set off as a separate town. In this way many towns have been repeatedly divided; at least eleven towns have been formed either in whole or in part from the original territory of the town of Dedham. At first the homes of the inhabitants were compactly centered about

[1] Martin, *The Evolution of the Massachusetts Public School System,* p. 74.

[2] Channing, *Town and County Government in the English Colonies of North America,* pp. 36, 37.

the mill, the school and the meeting house,[1] and each towns-
man had, not too distant for oversight, his acres of meadow,
upland, tillage, and woodland.[2]   But when concentration for
defense was no longer necessary the farming population
spread out over a wider area.   Many of the new agricultural
towns had no center of population, the homes of the inhabitants being widely scattered upon their respective farms.   In
others population was grouped about a number of isolated
hamlets, but there was no main nucleus of population.   It
now became inconvenient for all the townsmen to send their
children to a central school, or for them to attend a central
church.   Gradually, therefore, the town administration was
largely decentralized.   School districts, road districts and
parishes were formed, and many of the functions formerly
performed by the general town meeting were now turned
over to the inhabitants of the different districts.

The same movement is seen in the central administration.
The functions of the central administration were chiefly
military and judicial.   At first these matters were centrally
administered by the general court, the governor and his
assistants.   But as the settlements became scattered and
communication was very difficult, it was found inconvenient
to administer all these matters from a single center.   Accordingly the colony was divided, first into court districts,
then into military districts, and finally, in 1643, the shire or
county was formed.[3]   Legislation continued to be centralized,
but the laws centrally enacted were now administered by
local town and county officials.   The difficulties of transportation and communication were such that efficient central

---

[1] For better defense in case of attack by the Indians, the general court forbade
the building of dwellings distant more than half a mile from the meeting house.
Colony Records, v. 1, p. 181.

[2] Ellis, *Puritan Age in Mass.*, p. 253.

[3] Channing, *op. cit.*, pp. 34, 35.

control was out of the question. Decentralization came because under the conditions local administration was more efficient than central.[1]

Nevertheless this was a most unsatisfactory condition. The towns paid but little attention to many statutes of the legislature. In order to bring them under control, the statutes went more and more into detail, prescribing minutely the duties of each officer and affixing penalties for non-compliance. Nevertheless the enforcement of general laws continued practically to be a matter of local choice. But these detailed statutes had indirectly a very serious effect upon the position of the town. The town was originally not an authority of specific and enumerated powers, but of general powers. The towns at first sprang up and attended to the ordering of their own affairs without the authorization of the general court. The law of 1635 merely recognizes existing practices. It gives the towns control over their own organization and power to make "such orders as may concern the well ordering of their own towns, not repugnant to the laws and orders here established by the general court."[2] The towns were autonomous.

With the decentralization of the commonwealth administration and the consequent attempt to control local officials in the administration of general laws, all this was gradually changed. The detailed statutes definitely fixed the organization of the town and the duties of many of its officers. As the habit of legislative regulation grew stronger, the legislature no longer distinguished clearly between general interests and those which were purely local, but regulated all matters indiscriminately. The towns once autonomous gradually became so bound up in the meshes of detailed legislation

---

[1] In 1820 Maine, formerly a part of Massachusetts, became a separate state.

[2] *Colony Records*, v. I, p. 172.

that they could neither make any change in their organization nor undertake any new function without express authorization of the legislature. The town instead of being an authority of general powers became an authority of enumerated powers.[1]

2. *The Elimination of Distance and Centralization.* Early in the present century great dynamic forces were set at work, which were destined to bring about a complete reconstruction of the existing social structure. Of these, improvements in transportation and communication were the most vital. The movement began in Massachusetts with the construction of turnpikes between the larger towns ; then followed, in quick succession, the steamboat, the railroad and the telegraph. These were soon followed by the horse railway, cheap postage, the telephone, the electric railway and the bicycle. The tendency of the railroad, the telegraph and cheap and quick postal service was to bring about a concentration which was attended by the congestion of population in cities and the depopulation of the rural towns. The electric railway, the telephone and the bicycle came to counteract these evils ; while their tendency is strongly toward the centralization of business, it is also toward the diffusion of habitations.

These great socializing forces, going hand in hand with the development of the factory system and improvements in machinery, made possible a vastly higher organization of society than was possible under a stage-coach regime. The existing structure had to be transformed ; labor and capital had to be withdrawn from their isolated employments and concentrated in large centers, in order to reap the advantages

---

[1] The rule at present is that every exercise of authority on the part of a city or town must rest either on some express statutory provision, or upon long continued custom and usage. A few municipal powers have never become statutory; they are survivals of a time when the municipality had a general grant of power. See Spaulding *v.* Lowell, 23 Pickering, 71, 77, 78.

of the greater division of labor and co-operation now made possible. The result was a movement of labor and capital, of population and wealth, from the country to the city. Moreóver, in the localization of the agricultural industry, resulting from the opening up of the fertile plains of the West, many farmers were compelled to abandon their farms and move to the West or to the city. Since about 1860 many of the small towns have declined steadily; while the cities have grown as steadily and at a much more rapid rate. In 1890, 143 out of a total of 351 cities and towns, showed a smaller population than in 1865. There were 134 towns in which the annual product derived from agriculture exceeded that derived from manufactures; and these towns contained a population of 156,408 in 1865, and of 147,823 in 1890, a decline of 5.49 per cent.[1] The following table gives the number of towns showing a decline in population during each of the decennial periods, from 1865 to 1895:

Decennial Period.	Total number of cities and towns.	Towns showing a decline in population.	Aggregate decline.	Percentage decline.
1865–75	342	142	106,361	34.38
1875–85	348	153	34,675	13.10
1885–95	353	143	29,426	13.08

In 1790 less than five per cent. of the population lived in cities or towns of over twelve thousand; by 1855 the number had increased to forty per cent., and in 1895 it was sixty-five per cent. This is shown by the following table:

[1] Horace G. Wadlin, *The Growth of Cities in Massachusetts.* American Statistical Association Publications, v. 2, p. 166.

Year.	Number of cities and towns of more than 12,000 inhabitants.	Proportion of total population.	Year.	Number of cities and towns of more than 12,000 inhabitants.	Proportion of total population.
1790 ...	1	.048	1855 ...	14	.360
1800 ...	1	.058	1865 ...	15	.398
1810 ...	2	.098	1875 ...	19	.506
1820 ...	2	.107	1885 ...	27	.592
1830 ...	2	.123	1895 ...	32	.656
1840 ...	4	.191			

Economic reorganization necessitates political reorganization.

First. The economic organization has become vastly more complex, and manifestly the complexity of the political organization must keep pace with the complexity of the relations that it is its function to regulate. A countless number of new wants have arisen, most of which have been supplied by private enterprise, but many have required the direct or the indirect intervention of government. Under eighteenth century conditions the degree of technical and scientific knowledge required for both industrial and public administration was comparatively slight; now the highest technical and scientific service is required for the proper administration of both public and industrial affairs.

Second. Progress in the elimination of distance has tended toward centralization in public administration, no less than toward the centralization or organization of industry. The benefits of increased specialization can usually be obtained only by a more comprehensive organization, by a wider market or a larger administrative district.

Third. The circle of common interests has in many cases

been greatly extended. That which was the common interest of the district has become the common interest of the town; the common interest of the town has become that of a number of towns, or of the entire commonwealth; the common interest of the commonwealth has become that of a group of commonwealths or of the entire nation.

These changes demanded a complete political reorganization; a reorganization of the internal affairs of the municipalities and the commonwealth, a redistribution of functions between the municipalities and the commonwealth, and a readjustment of territorial lines. It was now that the movement that has been noted in the preceding period, the decentralization of state administration and the change in the position of the municipality from an authority of general to an authority of enumerated powers, became a factor of tremendous importance. This reorganization, which might have taken place with something of the ease and promptness with which the industrial reconstruction was effected, was effected but partially and tardily. The readjustment of the municipal organization demanded by the rapidly changing conditions, instead of taking place automatically with the changing needs of the municipality, was brought about, if at all, by the tardy and arbitrary methods of special legislation. The proper subjects of commonwealth administration and supervision had greatly increased; but the commonwealth, instead of directly administering or supervising these matters through its own officials, continued for a time its policy of devolving their administration upon local officials. The hands of both the municipalities and the commonwealth were thus effectually tied; neither was autonomous. The municipalities were dependent on the commonwealth legislature for the exercise of all legislative power; the commonwealth was dependent on municipal officials for the administration of its laws. Legislation was centralized and administration decentralized.

It is this condition that is believed to be a prime cause of the general disorganization throughout the United States, in commonwealth and especially in municipal government. This study of Massachusetts administration is presented because it is believed that this state has made the greatest progress towards a rational solution of the problem. As we have seen that the evil condition was brought about by the decentralized administration of matters of general concern and regarding which there was not a complete identity of interest between the municipality and the commonwealth, it is obvious that the first step in its removal must be a centralization in the administration of all such matters. Until this is done it is premature to demand municipal home rule; the legislature must continue to interfere continually in the organization and administration of municipal affairs. Massachusetts has made considerable progress in the direction of a more centralized administration; and with a clearer appreciation of the problem it would soon be ripe for the granting of a large sphere of autonomy to its municipalities.

CHAPTER II

PUBLIC SCHOOLS

THE evolution of the public school administration naturally divides itself into the two grand periods that have already been noted. During the first period there was little attempt at central regulation, and local control gradually passed from the towns to the districts. During the second period a considerable degree of central supervision and regulation has been developed and the district system has been abolished.

1. *Period of Decentralization.*

For nearly twenty years after the settlement of Salem in 1628, no law was passed by the general court relating to the establishment and maintenance of schools. Not until 1647 were the towns required, or even expressly authorized by law, to maintain schools. Yet previous to this time schools had been voluntarily established in all the principal towns. Boston established a school in 1635. The school system thus voluntarily established was soon recognized by the general court as a matter not purely of local but of general concern.

The school law of 1647 is concise but strong. It requires simply that each town of fifty householders shall maintain a school for the teaching of reading and writing, and that each town of one hundred householders shall maintain a school in which students may be fitted for Harvard College. With this general requirement, the demands of central control were satisfied: each town was left free to organize and manage its

school affairs in its own way.   The duty to maintain schools
was imposed on the town in its corporate capacity and not
upon any particular officer or board, and the schools could be
supported through fees, taxes or special funds.   This simple
law, with a few minor amendments, sets forth the relation of
the commonwealth to the public school for a period of one
hundred and forty-two years.

The enforcement of the law was left to the courts.   For
failure to maintain a grammar school, a penalty of five
pounds was imposed; the amount thus forfeited going to
the support of the nearest grammar school of an adjoining
town.   In 1671 the penalty was doubled.[1]   In 1701 the general court, after declaring the observance of the law "to be
shamefully neglected by divers towns, and the penalty therefore not required," again doubled the penalty; and it was
made the duty of county justices of the peace "to take effect-
ual care that the laws respecting schools and school-masters
be duly observed," and county grand juries were also specially charged with the enforcement of the law.[2]   Many of the
smaller towns felt the support of a grammar school to be an
unnecessary burden, and persistently refused to maintain it,
although repeatedly fined for their neglect.[3]   On June 17,
1718, the general court, after affirming that "by sad experience
it is found that many towns that not only are obliged by law,
but are very able to support a grammar school, yet choose
rather to incur and pay the fine or penalty than maintain a
grammar school," ordered that the penalty be greatly increased.[4]   This attempt was also unsuccessful, and in 1789
the requirements of the law were considerably reduced.

Development of the School District.   As has already been

---

[1] *Colony Records*, v. 4, p. 486.   [2] *Province Laws*, v. 1, p. 470.

[3] The grammar school, so-called, was really a preparatory school for Harvard
College.

[4] *Ibid.*, v. 2, p. 100.

noted, until about the beginning of the eighteenth century, the population of the town was compactly centered about the town meeting house.[1] Now a new epoch began. The settlers became widely scattered upon their respective farms. These new conditions made changes necessary in the former system, and the broad powers vested in the towns enabled them at once to meet these new demands without having to await the action of a distant legislature. As the children could no longer gather at a central school it was decided to send the school to them. The schoolmaster, instead of holding the school throughout the year at some central place, was now directed to teach for a certain portion of the year in each of several places. We thus have a moving or itinerant school. Gradually school houses were established in various places, the districts became well defined ; and the school tax levied by the town, instead of being expended under the direct supervision of the town meeting and the school committee, was apportioned among the several districts. Each district was allowed to draw its share of the school money and expend it as it saw fit. This latter stage was reached in some of the towns about the middle of the eighteenth century.[2]

In 1789,[3] this custom which had then existed in many of the towns for almost fifty years, was at length recognized and crystalized by legislative enactment. In 1800 school districts were given power to levy taxes for the erection and repair of school houses, but the power to tax for the maintenance of schools has always remained with the town.[4] In 1817 the district was made a corporation, with power to hold property, to sue and be sued.[5]

The development of the district system is usually condemned as an unmitigated evil ; the period in which it flourished is usually regarded as one of disintegration and

[1] See above, p. 11.   [2] Martin, *op. cit.*, p. 77.
[3] *Acts*, 1789, c. 19.   [4] *Ibid.*, 1799–1800, c. 66.   [5] *Ibid.*, 1817, c. 14.

degeneracy.   Yet it should be borne in mind that the argu-
ments that are now so convincing in favor of a more centralized system of school administration, have very little weight
when applied to eighteenth century conditions.   A more
centralized system is now favored, because with it a better
classification, and skilled instruction and supervision can be
secured, and the wealth of the richer districts can be drawn
upon to help bear the burdens of the poorer.   But in the
eighteenth century pedagogy was practically an unknown
science and skilled supervision an unknown art; while wealth
was much more evenly distributed than it is at present.
Centralization under such conditions would have been as
premature as would have been the organization of laborers
into large factories before machinery supplanted hand labor.
It would have been centralization merely for the sake of centralization, and would have been gained at the expense of
individual vigor and future progress.

2. *Period of Centralization.*

The law of 1789[1] was the most detailed school law that had
yet been enacted.   For the most part, however, it was simply
a codification of practices and customs that had been freely
developed in the towns and districts.   Early in the nineteenth
century there was a marked development of interest in education.   Industrial progress was attended by an increased
interest in social conditions.   The school problem began to
be more carefully studied, the importance of education to the
commonwealth as a whole began to be more generally recognized, and as a result legislative interference became more
and more frequent.

In 1826 each town was for the first time *required* to choose
a school committee, which was vested with the general supervision of all the schools of the town.[2]   Some member of the

---

[1] *Acts*, 1789, c. 19.   [2] *Ibid.*, 1825–26, c. 170.

committee was required to visit each school at least once a month, and the committee was required to make an annual report of school attendance, expenditure, etc., to the secretary of the commonwealth. In 1834 the school fund was established. The law provided for the accumulation of a fund of not more than one million dollars, the income of which was to be used for educational purposes.[1]

State Board of Education. The establishment of a school fund was but a beginning. A few men became convinced that the public school system of the time was deplorably deficient, that a campaign of education and enlightenment should be instituted, and that this work could best be performed by a state board of education. By an act approved April 20, 1837, the board of education was established. It was vested with no compulsory authority and simple duties, yet its advent was an epoch-making event in the history of education.

The board was to consist of the governor, the lieutenant-governor and eight members appointed by the governor with the consent of the council. The members were to receive no compensation but the board had power to appoint a paid secretary, who was to be its executive officer. The organization of the board has since remained unchanged. Its duties, most of which were actually to be performed through its secretary, were (1) to prepare an abstract of the school returns made by the local committees; (2) to "collect information of the actual condition and efficiency of the common schools;" (3) "to diffuse as widely as possible throughout every part of the commonwealth, information of the most approved and successful methods of arranging the studies and conducting the education of the young;" (4) to make an annual report to the legislature upon the condition

---

[1] *Acts*, 1834, c. 169.

of the schools and the most practical means of improving
them.   Soon afterwards the board was given power to prescribe the form of school registers, and of the returns and
reports of school committees, and to see that the towns before receiving their portion of the state school fund, fulfilled
the requirements of the law with respect to returns, taxation
and maintenance of schools.   Cities, which have recently
been required to provide instruction in manual training, must
obtain the board's approval of the course provided.[1]

It is seen, therefore, that the control which the board exercises over local school authorities is very small indeed.
It is very weak as compared with the extensive powers exercised by state superintendents and boards in many other
states.   The board has no compulsory authority over the
certification of teachers and no legal power to decide appeals
and settle disputes between local officials.   But diplomas
from the state normal schools under the management of the
board, and certificates granted by the board, may be accepted
by the local school committees in lieu of a local examination.
Moreover, "the services of the board as a voluntary arbiter
in school questions are often sought.   These questions are
frequently brought before the secretary or agents of the
board; both parties in an educational dispute gladly avail-
ing themselves of the advice or decision which they thus
receive."[2]

The chief function of the board has ever been to advise,
enlighten and arouse, but not to compel.   It was with this
conception of the true sphere of the board that Horace
Mann, its first secretary, took up the work.   With an
enthusiasm that has seldom been equaled he began a campaign of education.   The means that he employed were pub-

[1] *Acts,* 1894, c. 471.

[2] *Report of the Board of Education,* 1895, p. 11.

lic conventions, meetings, the press, pamphlets and reports. He speaks of his task as follows:[1]

"The education of the whole people, in a republican government, can never be attained without the consent of the whole people. Compulsion, even if it were desirable, is not an available instrument. Enlightenment, not coercion, is our resource. The nature of education must be explained. The whole mass of mind must be instructed in regard to its comprehension and enduring interests. We can not drive our people up a dark avenue, even though it be the right one; but we must hang the starry lights of knowledge about it and show them not only the directness of its course to the goal of prosperity and honor, but the beauty of the way that leads to it."

In 1850 the board was authorized to appoint agents to assist the secretary. Their main duties have been to visit schools, advise teachers, superintendents and school committees, and to deliver educational addresses. They have sometimes been called upon to address town meetings. At present the board has four agents. Mr. George A. Walton, for twenty-five years an agent of the board, says of their work:

"With the present force there exist the most intimate personal relations between the several town school officials and the agents, and hence, indirectly with the secretary of the Board. The most obscure village in the most out-of-the-way district of the state can be reached by a representative of the Board with a day's notice. Probably there is no State in the Union where the actual condition of all the public schools is so open and apparent to the State Superintendent as are ours to the secretary of the State Board. It is doubtful if in any state having a system of county superintendents

---

[1] *Life and Works of Horace Mann*, ii, p. 286; iii, p. 2.

school interests have been as vitally affected by their supervision as have those of Massachusetts by the counsel and
instruction of the agents in the last ten years."[1]

A most important function of the board has been to serve
as professional adviser of the legislature. It has repeatedly
made investigations at the instance of the legislature. The
legislature has seldom taken any important step in school
legislation without a special report on the subject from the
board. The secretary and members of the board have always
stood ready to give legislative committees the benefit of their
greater experience and trained judgment, and their advice
has usually been sought. As the central control over local
school authorities has thus far been almost entirely legislative, the function of the board in this connection has been
one of prime importance.

When the board began its work in 1837, there were practically no professionally-trained teachers in the schools. The
development of a trained teaching force, supervised by
trained superintendents, has been a work that has constantly
engaged the best efforts of the board. Through its influence
ten state normal schools have been opened: two in 1839,
one in 1840, 1854, 1873 and 1874, and four in 1897. In
1896 about one-third of the teachers in the public schools
had received a professional training in these schools. They
are under the direct control of the board. The teachers'
institute is another means used by the board for the education of teachers. Attendance at the institutes is voluntary.
The expense is paid by the state, and they are held under
the direction of the agents of the board.[2]

The Downfall of the District System. But the establishment of normal schools and institutes was the easiest part of

---

[1] *Report of the Board of Education,* 1895–96, p. 239.

[2] *Acts,* 1846, c. 99.

the problem. To secure the employment of trained teachers by the local authorities and their supervision by trained superintendents, was a much more difficult task. A prime requisite in the securing of professionally-trained officials is that their appointment and tenure be based entirely on merit; but instead of this being the case, appointment and tenure were usually based on kinship or friendship to a constantly changing district committeeman. Nor could efficient supervision be obtained under the district system. Each district could not afford to employ a trained superintendent for its single teacher. Moreover, with progress in the art of teaching, just as with progress in every other art or industry, specialization became necessary. In place of one teacher, teaching all grades and all subjects, modern methods require a special teacher for each grade and in some cases for each subject. This, too, is an impossibility under the district system. In any undertaking the benefits of increased specialization can usually be secured only by a more comprehensive organization. The enlargement of the local unit of school administration was, therefore, a problem of fundamental importance.

At the time the board of education began its work in 1837, the district system was almost universal. A few of the more compact and progressive towns, however, had never adopted the district system. As a rule there was but a single school in each district. The appointment and removal of the teacher were in the hands of a prudential committeeman elected by the district. The teachers appointed had first to be approved by the town committee, but this was usually merely a matter of form. Although the town could abolish the district system altogether, or if it saw fit, exercise a very strong control over the districts, in practice the districts were given the greatest possible freedom.

In 1838[1] a law was passed providing that the town school committee should contract with the teachers of the district schools unless the town, by a special vote in town meeting, decided that this power should be retained by the prudential committee. In the same year any two districts were authorized to unite for the purpose of supporting a school for the more advanced pupils.[2] In 1844 the town school committee was authorized to remove any district teacher.[3] In 1853 the school committee was empowered to discontinue the districts unless the town voted triennially for their continuance;[4] but in 1857 the law was repealed.[5] In 1859 the district system was summarily abolished,[6] but at a special session of the same year the repealing act was itself as summarily repealed. Ten years later, in 1869,[7] the system was again abolished, only to be partially reëstablished the next year by a law authorizing it upon a two-thirds vote of the town.[8] Not until 1882 was its final overthrow accomplished, and at that time it had already been voluntarily abandoned by all but forty-five towns.[9]

Skilled Supervision. The district system abolished, the next step was to place the schools of the town under the supervision of a trained superintendent. The first general law authorizing the employment of superintendents by town and city school committees was that of 1854.[10] But previous to this Springfield had temporarily tried the experiment in 1840. In all, ninety-four cities and towns have taken advantage of this act.[11] This number consists of the cities and the larger towns. To the small rural and urban towns with but

[1] *Acts*, 1838, c. 105. [2] *Ibid.*, 1838, c. 189.
[3] *Ibid.*, 1844, c. 32. [4] *Ibid.*, 1853, c. 153.
[5] *Ibid.*, 1857, c. 254. [6] *Ibid.*, 1859, c. 252.
[7] *Ibid.*, 1869, c. 110. [8] *Ibid.*, 1870. c. 196.
[9] *Ibid.*, 1882, c. 219. [10] *Ibid.*, 1854, c. 314.
[11] *Report of the Board of Education*, 1895–96, p. 89.

few schools, the expense of skilled superintendence appeared too great. To remedy this difficulty a law was passed in 1870 permitting two or more towns to unite for the purpose of employing a superintendent. Only seventeen towns, however, were formed into districts under this provision. Many doubtless would have been inclined to do so had they not been dissuaded by the somewhat difficult task of coming to an agreement with other towns. Moreover many of these small rural towns have been steadily declining in population and wealth. This being the case, progressive action on their part, especially if it involves an increase in the tax rate, can hardly be expected. To overcome this difficulty, a law offering state aid to such districts as should be formed was passed in 1888. This law as amended in 1893 provides that any two or more towns, "the valuation of each of which does not exceed two million five hundred thousand dollars, and the aggregate number of schools in all of which is not more than fifty nor less than twenty-five," uniting into a district for the purpose of employing a superintendent, shall annually receive $1,250 from the state. One hundred and fifty-one towns have taken advantage of this act. Altogether the schools of 262 cities and towns, out of a total of 353, are now under skilled superintendents, and in these schools are 93.8 per cent. of the school children of the state. Ninety-one towns are still without superintendents. The board of education holds that voluntary action has now about reached its limit, and that it is time for the state to use its compulsory authority to form these remaining towns into districts for the employment of superintendents.[1]

Consolidation of the Weaker Schools. While this process of centralization in the control and supervision of the schools has been going on, a similar process has been taking place

[1] *Report of Board of Education*, 1896–97.

in the schools themselves. The feebler schools are being consolidated. This consolidation has been made practicable by the towns undertaking to pay for the conveyance of children living at a distance from the school. A law authorizing this was passed in 1869. The development of electric roads has greatly hastened the movement. In recent years the expenditure for conveyance has rapidly increased; in 1889 it was $22,118; in 1897 it was $105,317. Its effects may be seen from the fact that while, in the last two years, the number of school class-rooms shows an increase of 683, the total number of schools shows a decrease of 89. This is perhaps the beginning of the end of the little red school-house.

Legislative Regulation. The commonwealth has almost from the start prescribed a certain minimum of school facilities to be maintained by the localities. During the period at present under consideration, this minimum has been repeatedly increased. Aside from the increased requirements as to studies and the length of the school year, the cities and towns have been required to furnish free text-books, and the larger cities and towns have been required to provide evening schools and manual training schools. It is interesting to note the very gradual way in which this control has developed. It has not been used to introduce new methods into the schools of the state, but to universalize existing methods. All of the improvements and reforms which have finally been made compulsory and universal, have been first adopted voluntarily by the more progressive and enterprising cities.[1]

Independent Position of the School Committee. An important fact in the development of central control has been the transference from the town or city in its corporate capacity

[1] See Martin, *op. cit.*, p. 268.

to the school committee, of almost the entire local control and authority in regard to schools. Down to 1826, the town was not required to elect a school committee.[1] The duty of maintaining schools was imposed upon the town in its corporate capacity, and the administration of school affairs might be attended to by the town meeting itself, or delegated to the selectmen, or to a special school committee. As a matter of fact a school committee was usually appointed, but it was entirely under the control of the town meeting.

Nineteenth century legislation has wrought a complete change in the relation of the school committee to the town meeting and the city council. New powers and duties have almost invariably been vested in the school committee instead of in the town or city in its corporate capacity, as was formerly the case. Practically the only control retained by the city council and town meeting is a limited control over the expenditure of money for school purposes.[2]

In the words of the supreme court, "The power given to the school committee to contract with teachers necessarily implies and includes the power to determine their salaries. And in so doing they are not restricted to the amount appropriated by the city council."[3] The city council merely appropriates a gross sum for the maintenance of schools, and the work of apportioning this sum for different purposes is performed by the school committee; but the committee does not hesitate to make expenditures considerably in excess of its appropriations. This divided financial responsibility leads to constant friction between the city council and the school committee, and the placing of the schools in the charge of a superintendent or board appointed by the mayor is being

[1] See above, p. 22.

[2] Roberts *v.* Boston, 5 Cushing, 198, 207.

[3] Charlestown *v.* Gardner, 98 Mass., 587.

agitated.[1]   In some cities the school committee is the only
survival of the independent board system of city government.

The School Fund.   The dominant idea in the establishment
of the school fund in 1834 was neither to relieve the local governments of the support of schools, nor to bring about a more
equitable distribution of school burdens by taxing the
wealthier localities for the benefit of the poorer.   It was established as the most unobjectionable and practicable means
of introducing a small amount of central supervision and
control.[2]   Perhaps the most definite object in view was the
securing of reports and returns from the local school committees.   In 1826, school committees were required to make
annual reports to the secretary of the commonwealth, but, as
no penalty was provided, few towns responded.   In 1832,
ninety-nine towns out of a total of three hundred and five
made returns; in 1833, but eighty-five reported.   It was
largely for the purpose of correcting this evil that the school
fund was established in 1834.   No town can receive any part
of the income of the fund that does not make the returns required by law.[3]

Almost from the start, moreover, the receiving of state aid
has been conditioned upon the raising of a certain minimum
amount by local taxation.   In 1836 this minimum was fixed
at one dollar for each child of school age.[4]   In 1839 the
minimum was raised to $1.25,[5] in 1849 to $1.50,[6] and in 1865
to $3.00.[7]   In this year, also, the fulfillment of the provisions
of the law in regard to the number of schools and the length
of the school year was included among the requirements for

---

[1] Matthews, *The City Government of Boston,* p. 15; *Mayor Quincy's Message,*
Jan. 3, 1898, pp. 20–27.

[2] See the report of the house committee, *House Doc.* 16, 1833.

[3] *Acts,* 1835, c. 138.   [4] *Revised Statutes,* c. 23, § 66, 1836.

[5] *Acts,* 1839, c. 56.   [6] *Ibid.,* 1849, c. 117.   [7] *Ibid.,* 1865, c. 142.

the receipt of state aid;[1] and in 1878 the enforcement of the truancy laws by the local authorities was also added.[2]

Distribution of the School Fund.   At first the idea of making use of the school fund to equalize the burden of school support does not appear to have been considered.   At the time of its establishment wealth was comparatively equally distributed; the disparity in the per capita wealth of the various communities, which has now become so enormous, had scarcely begun to develop.   Nevertheless, the method of distribution from the start has been one which has *tended* to counteract existing inequalities.   The law of 1835[3] provides for its distribution in proportion to population, and the amount of taxes raised for school purposes.   In the following year the number of children of school age was made the basis and so continued until 1866.

But notwithstanding the method of distribution the amount of the school fund was so small that its effect as an equalizer was very slight indeed.   In 1836, the total amount distributed among the towns was but $16,230.57, and in 1870 but $70,637.62.   In 1866 the first step towards the relief of the small towns was taken.   By this act, each city and town first received seventy-five dollars and the remainder was distributed as formerly in proportion to the number of children of school age.[4]   This afforded but slight relief, however, and the secretary of the board of education in his report for 1872 dwells at length on the inequality in the school burdens of the various towns.[5]   He calls attention to the recent marked development in this inequality; producing statistics to show that during the past six years the richest communities had been growing richer, and the poorest had as a rule been

---

[1] *Acts*, 1865, c. 142.   [2] *Ibid.*, 1878, c. 234.   [3] *Ibid.*, 1835, c. 138.

[4] *Ibid.*, 1866, c. 208.   In 1869 the law was amended so as to give each town one hundred dollars instead of seventy-five.

[5] *35th Report of the Board of Education*, pages 117–132.

growing poorer. It had become practically impossible for the poorer towns to provide adequate educational advantages. He recommended that a state half-mill tax be levied, and the proceeds distributed to the various towns in proportion to the number of children of school age.[1]

Although the secretary's plan for a half-mill tax was not carried out, its agitation led to a revision of the method of distributing the school fund in 1874.[2] By this law all towns with a valuation exceeding ten million dollars, were deprived of their share in the school fund. In 1875 the valuation of eighteen of the largest cities and towns in the state exceeded this amount. This principle of using the school fund for the benefit of those towns whose needs are greatest was further extended in 1891. By this law the entire amount is distributed among the towns that have a valuation of not to exceed three million dollars. In 1896 the valuation of ninety-eight cities and towns, containing 82.2 per cent. of the population of the state,[3] exceeded this amount, and they consequently received no part of the income of the school fund. Since they receive no aid, the state control, which in the case of the other towns is imposed as a condition of state aid, does not exist. But this is of no practical importance, as the conditions upon which state aid is granted are so simple that they are voluntarily complied with by all but the poorest and most unprogressive towns.

Special Aid to Poor Towns. Aside from the distribution of half the income of the school fund among the poorer towns, the state grants them various special aids. We have already noted the law of 1888 by which unions of two or more towns of a valuation of not exceeding two million five

---

[1] A half-mill tax upon the valuation of 1871 would have yielded $748,675.84. In the same year the amount raised by local taxation for ordinary school expenses was $3,272,335.33.

[2] *Acts*, 1874, c. 348.   [3] According to the census of 1895.

hundred thousand dollars are assisted in the employment of a superintendent.[1] By the law of 1896, as amended in 1897, towns of less than $350,000 valuation are assisted in the payment of teachers.[2] By a law of 1895, any town whose valuation does not exceed $500,000 and which does not maintain a high school, is entitled to be reimbursed by the state for the expenses of transportation and tuition of children of the town attending the high school of another town.[3]

A similar policy has been adopted by the state in aiding the poorer towns in the establishment of free public libraries. In 1890 there were 103 towns in which there were no free libraries. They were almost without exception small towns with a slender valuation, and in 67 of them there had been a decline in population during the preceding five years.[4] The law of 1890, as amended in 1892, provides for the appointment of a free public library commission.[5] It is the duty of this commission to give advice to local librarians and trustees, and to expend one hundred dollars in the purchase of books for each town that will establish a library and annually appropriate a certain amount for its support. The commission is also authorized a expend a like amount in aid of any town whose valuation does not exceed six hundred thousand dollars, that already maintained a free library previous to 1890, under similar conditions with respect to an annual town appropriation. As a result of this policy, there are at present but ten towns, containing but three-fifths of one per cent. of the population of the state, without free library privileges.[6]

The state, therefore, evidently recognizes a dependent

[1] See above, p. 29.   [2] *Acts*, 1896, 408; *Acts*, 1897, 498.   [3] *Acts*, 1895, 212.

[4] Tillinghast, *The Free Public Libraries of Mass.*, p. 4. Published in the *Fifty-fourth Report of the Board of Education.*

[5] *Acts*, 1890, 347; *Acts*, 1892, 255.

[6] *Report of the Free Public Library Commission*, 1897.

class of municipalities. It recognizes that towns that are steadily growing poorer, that each recurring census finds with a decreased population and valuation, stand in need of special aid and control. The cities and the large growing towns can be relied upon to provide for education in an adequate and satisfactory manner. The larger cities have always been the first to adopt new methods; it is here that specialization and organization in educational methods have been most highly perfected. It has been the policy of the state, through the efforts and authority of the board of education, through compulsory laws, and through financial assistance, to bring to the poorer rural towns the methods which have already been voluntarily adopted and tested in the larger and more progressive cities and towns. State control is here primarily a problem of the country and not of the city.

Conclusion. Except in the case of the dependent class of towns there does not appear to be any great demand for increased legislative or administrative control. The main field of the state board, aside from its control over these towns that are the recipients of state aid, would seem to lie (1) in collecting statistics and information for the use of the local authorities and of the state legislature; (2) in undertaking investigations for the legislature and in serving as its professional adviser; (3) in giving advice and counsel to local authorities, (4) in establishing schools and institutes for the professional training of teachers, and (5) in the examination and certification of teachers. Its function is predominantly that of rendering services to the localities rather than the exercise of direct control over them. But this condition may be modified.

We have already followed the enlargement of the local unit of school administration from the district to the town and from the town to a union of towns under a single superintendent. We have seen that this centralization has been the result of two forces, (1) the desire to equalize the burden of school support, and (2) the desire to secure the benefits of classification and special training.

1. Whether the demands of increased classification and special training require any further centralization is doubtful. Were higher education a governmental function in Massachusetts it would undoubtedly be a function of the state government. Secondary education is in a more doubtful position. Many small towns do not attempt to maintain high schools, and in others the high schools are weak and inefficient. Here there is a demand for consolidation; for an enlargement of the unit of administration. The state has already done something to obviate the difficulty by paying for the tuition and transportation of children of a town in which there is no high school, attending the high school of a neighboring town.[1] Secondary education may become the field of a considerable amount of central administrative control. As to elementary education, the interests of classification and special training do not at present appear to demand any further centralization in its administration.

2. That the desire to equalize the burden of school support will lead to further centralization is more probable. In the distribution of its school fund the policy of Massachusetts differs materially from that of other states. Instead of distributing a very large amount of money in proportion to wealth or population to all its cities and towns, Massachusetts distributes a very small amount among those towns only that are unable to provide adequate educational facilities. But as the entire fund distributed in 1897 amounted to but $86,968.95, while the total amount raised by local taxation for ordinary school expenses was $7,736,815.48, it will be

---

[1] See above, p. 35.

seen that state aid does very little toward overcoming the great disparity in the ability of the various communities to support schools. The demand that this inequality shall be equalized by a state school tax has therefore become strong and persistent.[1] If this movement is successful it will probably be followed by increased central administrative control. If the state collects a general tax, it cannot relieve itself of the responsibility for its proper application.

What then is the true relation of the commonwealth to the public school? In the first place, it must be recognized that the school system is a matter in which the entire commonwealth is vitally interested. This has been continuously recognized ever since the law of 1647, imposing upon the towns the obligation of maintaining schools. In this capacity, therefore, the municipality acts as the agent of the commonwealth. It performs a service for the commonwealth. Its position is, in this respect, analogous to that of a railroad corporation—a private corporation for the performance of a public function.

This being the case, the question of direct central management or of central supervision will turn largely upon whether there is or is not a substantial identity between the interests of the municipality in the maintenance of schools and the interests of the commonwealth. If their interests are entirely antagonistic, direct central management is the logical solution. The strongest kind of central administrative supervision will not suffice to bring about the most efficient management. If their interests are identical in most and antagonistic in but a few respects, a more or less extensive degree of central control is probably the best solution. In school administration the interests of most of the municipalities are substantially identical with those of the commonwealth. It

[1] In 1897 a bill providing for a mill school tax passed the legislature, but was vetoed by the governor.

is only in the decaying, dependent towns that even a slight antagonism can be said to exist.   There, a considerable degree of central control is doubtless required. As to the other cities and towns, the function of the state board would seem to lie in aiding them, as at present, with information and advice, in inspecting their work and requiring reports in the interest of publicity, and in directly interfering only in occasional cases of gross neglect of duty.   Though it is probably expedient to give the state board very broad powers over the local authorities, in order to avoid the necessity of detailed statutes or special legislation, a very sparing use of such powers is most desirable.   Under such a system local interest in the schools is preserved.   The system is not reduced to uniformity and rigidity.   That inequality exists in school conditions, which is the greatest incentive to improvement and progress.   Each municipality profits by the successes and failures of its neighbors.   All the benefits of a healthy individualism are secured.

CHAPTER III

PUBLIC POOR RELIEF

IN this chapter it is proposed to show the evolution in public charity organization. In the first period of development, effective organization is almost entirely lacking; the central authority is exercised as much in the interest of town independence as of real central control. Here will be noted the laws making it increasingly difficult to gain a " settlement " in any town, and the consequent development of a class of "state paupers." Then the movement toward a better organization will be followed, showing the less stringent settlement laws, central administrative supervision, and the beginnings of a more scientific differentiation between the state and the towns of the work of caring for the poor.

1. *Period of Decentralization.*

Previous to 1639 the towns appear to have done just as they pleased in the matter of the admission of persons to a settlement. Each town took care that no one who seemed likely to become a public charge was admitted. In 1639 the general court gave to any two magistrates the power to determine all differences concerning the settling of poor persons, and " power to dispose of all unsettled persons into such towns as they shall judge to be most fit for the maintenance of such persons and the most ease of the country." In 1655 there was a return to the former system, each town being authorized to refuse admission to persons coming from other towns, and new comers might be warned to depart at any time until they were formally admitted as inhabitants.   Four years afterwards this law was amended by providing that any person might gain a settlement by residing for three months in a town, without having been warned to depart by the selectmen or constable.   The county court was empowered to hear all disputes as to place of settlement, and in case the place of settlement could not be determined, the poor person in question was to be left in the town where found, and the expense of his keeping to be paid for out of the county treasury.   In 1701 the term of residence necessary to gain a settlement was lengthened from three months to one year.   Finally in 1766 it was made impossible for a person to gain a settlement by any length of residence.   A person desiring to become an inhabitant of any town must make known his wish to the selectmen, and his application must be approved by a vote of the inhabitants assembled in town meeting.[1]

The towns were required to relieve all the poor persons whom they permitted to acquire settlements.   Naturally, therefore, they were very cautious in extending to new comers the right to a settlement.   Nevertheless, as there was little immigration, the number of persons without a settlement was very small.   These, in case of need, were at first, as we have seen, relieved by the towns at the expense of the county.   But soon the class known as "state paupers" began to develop.   As early as 1675 the relief of the unsettled poor at the expense of the central government finds a precedent.   As a result of King Philip's war many settlements had been broken up and their inhabitants forced to seek refuge in other towns.   The general court therefore ordered that these refugees should not thereby gain a settlement in the town, and in case they required relief the ex-

[1] Cummings, *Poor Laws of Massachusetts and New York*, Pub. Am. Econ. Association, vol. x., no. 4, pp. 21–34.

pense to the town should be reimbursed from the public treasury.[1]   The law of 1701 regulating immigration provides that sick immigrants shall be relieved by the towns at the expense of the province.[2]   Relief by the towns at the expense of the province is also provided for by a law of the same year in the case of unsettled poor persons falling sick with contagious diseases.[3]   Again, in 1766, it is provided that poor persons who have a settlement in some other American colony shall be conveyed through the various towns by their respective constables to the border of the province, and that each town shall be reimbursed for its expense by the province.[4]   Finally, in the laws of 1789 and 1794, a state pauper class is definitely recognized.   All unsettled paupers are to be relieved by the towns at the expense of the commonwealth.[5]

The act of 1794 also made important changes in the settlement law.   The law of 1766 had provided that no one could gain a settlement except by vote of the town.   The act of 1794 shows a slight advance.   It provides several other methods by which a settlement may be gained, the most important of which is that of continuous residence for ten years and the payment of all taxes for any five years thereof.   The conditions of the time, however, demanded a much more liberal measure.   A considerable immigration was setting in and improved roads made a freer movement of population inevitable.   Yet this law, though ill-adapted to the comparatively immobile conditions of that time, remained practically unchanged down to 1865 ; adapted only to a condition of status, it remained unchanged during an age of railways.

[1] See the *Report of the State Board of Charities*, 1864, p. 236.

[2] *Province Laws*, v. 1, p. 452.

[3] *Ibid.*, v. 1, p. 469.   [4] *Ibid.*, v. 4, p. 911.

[5] Law of Jan. 10, 1789; Law of Feb. 26, 1794.

With a considerable immigration, developing manufactures and a stringent settlement law, it is not surprising that the number of unsettled or state paupers increased rapidly. Between 1792 and 1820 the expense for state paupers increased five-fold, while the population did not double.[1] Previous to 1820 the commonwealth reimbursed the towns for the actual amount spent by them in the support of state paupers; but in this year the maximum state allowance per week for an adult pauper was fixed at one dollar, and in the following year it was further reduced to ninety cents.[2] During the next five years, owing to these measures and to the separation of the district of Maine from Massachusetts, the expense for state paupers decreased, but during the following five years again began to increase. By 1832 the number of state paupers had become almost as great as the number of town paupers.[3] Accordingly, the state allowance was again cut down. It became seventy cents a week for each adult pauper in 1831, and four years later it was reduced to forty-nine cents.[4]

Though by this means the legislature was successful in keeping down the commonwealth's expenditure for the state poor, their number increased more rapidly than ever. This condition was the result of the settlement law which was framed to meet the wants of a comparatively fixed population, but its evil results were greatly increased by the irresponsible method adopted in relieving the unsettled poor. They were relieved by the towns in which they happened to

[1] The payments to the towns for the support of state paupers amounted to $14,424.71 in 1793, and $72,662.54 in 1820. See the *Report of the Committee on the Pauper Laws*, 1821.

[2] *Report of the Commissioners on the Pauper System*, 1833, p. 13.

[3] The number of state poor is given as 5,927, and the number of town poor as 6,063. *Ibid.*, p. 13.

[4] Cummings, *op. cit.*, p. 42.

be, and each town sent in its account to be allowed by the legislature.

Many of the towns had no almshouses or poor farms, and were in the habit of disposing of their poor at auction to the lowest bidder. The state poor were therefore farmed out by the state to the towns, and then sub-farmed by the towns to contractors. It was charged, moreover, that this method was largely responsible for the development of a large "wandering poor" or tramp class.[1] There was no central supervision over the town officials, and in fact no thorough investigation and audit of the accounts which they presented to the state for payment. Many towns took advantage of this to profit at the state's expense. In 1836 a legislative committee reports that Cambridge, by employing a large number of able-bodied foreigners at road labor and in "a large establishment," and by drawing from the state an annual sum for their support, secures enough revenue to sustain its own paupers, and in addition yield a net profit of about two thousand dollars a year.[2] As a result of another legislative investigation, "it was found that dead paupers had been charged for as living; that, during the suspension of work, whole manufacturing villages had been enrolled as state paupers; that in some small towns trifling gifts to families were made the basis of charging all their members to the state for the entire winter. Many other similar impositions were discovered."[3]

2. *Period of Centralization.*

Largely as a result of these disclosures a board of "commissioners of alien passengers and state paupers" was established in 1851. It was vested with the administration of the

---

[1] *Report of the Commissioners on the Pauper System,* 1833, pp. 14–23.

[2] *House Document,* 41, 1836, p. 4.

[3] *Report State Board of Health, Lunacy and Charity,* 1881, p. cxxviii.

immigration laws and the supervision of the town authorities
in the care of state paupers.   For the latter purpose it was
authorized to appoint agents to visit at least once a year all
almshouses and places where state paupers were supported,
in order to see that the laws were regarded and to prevent
the towns from imposing on the commonwealth in their accounts for the support of state paupers.[1]   The commissioners
saved $22,330.80 to the commonwealth during the first year
by disallowing the illegal claims of the towns, and reduced
the number of state paupers from 16,154 to 10,267.[2]

In 1863 the board of alien commissioners was abolished
and its duties transferred to the state board of charities then
established.[3] This board was given a general supervision
over the state charitable and correctional institutions.   In
1879 the state boards of charity and health were consolidated
under the name of the state board of health, lunacy and
charity.   In 1886 this board was divided into a board of
health and a board of lunacy and charity.   A recent commission has recommended the establishment of a separate
state board of insanity and of a department for children.[4]
As at present organized the board consists of nine unsalaried
members appointed by the governor and council for terms of
five years.   They cannot be removed by the governor and
council, and the system of partial renewal is adopted.[5]

The Care of the Poor in State Institutions. The alien commissioners in their first report recommended the erection of
state almshouses for the care of the unsettled or state poor.
Their recommendations were adopted by the legislature and

---

[1] *Acts*, 1851, 342.

[2] Sanborn, *The Public Charities of Massachusetts*, 1776–1876, p. cxcvii.

[3] *Acts*, 1863, 240.

[4] *Report of the Commission to Investigate the Public Charitable and Reformatory Interests and Institutions of the Commonwealth*, 1897.

[5] *Acts*, 1879, 291; *Acts*, 1886, 101.

three state almshouses were opened in 1854. The expectations of the supporters of a system of state almshouses were not fully realized. The number of state paupers continued to increase and the expense to the commonwealth was increased rather than diminished. The poor in the state almshouses were, however, upon the whole better provided for than the town poor, and some attempt at classification was made. Many people, however, were of the opinion that poor relief could best be administered by the town authorities, who were better acquainted with the needs of the poor; and it was argued that removal to a state institution usually meant permanent pauperization. A special joint committee of the legislature reported that the state almshouses ought not to be permanently maintained, and a minority of the committee were in favor either of an immediate return to the old system, or of the adoption of a system requiring "each town and city to support all of the paupers residing within their own respective municipalities."[1]

The state almshouses were not abolished, but their importance has been considerably diminished by successive legislative acts, by which the administration of relief to a great number of the unsettled poor has again devolved upon the towns, while the number of unsettled poor has also been greatly reduced by changes in the settlement law.

The abuses that arose from the transportation of sick paupers to a state almshouse, led in 1865 to the enactment of a law providing that the towns be allowed three dollars a week for the support of sick state paupers.[2] The necessity of removing all state poor to the state almshouses often led to the permanent pauperization of a person or family where a little temporary aid locally administered would have

[1] Report of the special joint committee on public charitable institutions, *Senate Documents*, no. 2, 1859.

[2] *Acts*, 1865, 162.

sufficed. Accordingly a law was passed permitting the local
authorities to grant temporary aid to state paupers, but only
under the strict supervision of the state board of charities.[1]
The number thus temporarily supported by the towns was
30,363 in 1897, while the total number of state poor in state
institutions was but 3,199.[2]

In 1865 it was estimated that half of the people of the
state had no settlement in any of its cities or towns. Many,
moreover, though having a settlement, had it in some other
city or town than the one in which they were living.[3] Prior
to 1865 no material change had been made in the settlement
laws since 1794. In that year a " military settlement " law
was passed. As subsequently amended, it declares that any
person who has enlisted in the service of the United States
during the Civil War, as a part of the quota of any city or
town, has thereby gained a settlement in that city or town.
In 1874 the law was so amended that any person residing in
a place five years, and paying all taxes for any three years
thereof, gained a settlement. Several other more unimport-
ant amendments have been made at various times. As a result, the proportion of persons in the state having no settlement has been greatly reduced. The average number of
state poor in institutions was 2,591 in 1865, and 3,199 in
1897, while during the same period the average number of
city and town poor in institutions increased from 3,361 to
8,304.[4] The recent special commission recommends a

---

[1] *Acts*, 1877, 183; *Acts*, 1891, 90.

[2] See the *Report of the State Board of Lunacy and Charity*, 1897, pp. xliv., xlv.

[3] A settlement once gained in a Massachusetts town continues, and descends to
offspring through succeeding generations, and is only defeated by the gaining of
a settlement in another town in the state. *Report of the Board of Health, Lunacy
and Charity*, 1880, p. xix.

[4] *Report of the State Board of Lunacy and Charity*, 1897, p. xliv.

further amendment of the law, providing that a settlement may be gained by a continuous residence of three years.[1]

While the experiment of state almshouses was not entirely successful, and there has since 1865 been a considerable decentralization in the administration of ordinary poor relief, there has also been a movement toward a centralized administration of certain special kinds of relief, particularly the care of dependent children and of the insane poor.

Aside from the juvenile offenders, the state board had under its direct control in 1897 1,822 dependent children. This number consists of all abandoned, neglected or dependent infants under three years of age ; and of neglected or dependent children between three and sixteen years of age, growing up without salutary control, who have no legal settlement.   512 children are cared for by the various cities and towns.   The state board recommends that all neglected and dependent children under sixteen years of age be maintained at the expense of the state and under its direct control.[2]

Of the 6,702 pauper insane in 1897, 5,279 were in state asylums or boarded in families under state cotrol; 431 were in city asylums; 939 were in town almshouses and 53 in families under town control.   The state bears the expense of caring for the unsettled poor, but the cities and towns pay the state for caring for their settled poor in the state asylums. On account of the expense of keeping their poor insane in state institutions, many towns keep their harmless chronically insane in their almshouses.   Often in this way the sane are kept with the insane with no attempt at separation.   In order to aid the small towns in maintaining their insane poor in state asylums, an act of 1892 provides that towns having an assessed valuation of less than $500,000 may be partly or

---

[1] *Report of the Commission on Charitable and Reformatory Interests*, 1897, p. 35.

[2] See the *Report of the Commission on Charitable and Reformatory Interests*, 1897, p. 8; *Report of the State Board of Lunacy and Charity*, 1897, pp. 186–7.

wholly reimbursed for the support of their insane by the state. In 1897, forty-seven towns received aid under this provision. The law leaves it to the governor and council to determine what proportion of the expense shall be reimbursed; and, by their recent ruling, towns having a valuation of less than $200,000 are allowed their expenses in full; towns having a valuation of between $200,000 and $300,000, three-quarters of their expenses; and towns having a valuation of between $300,000 and $500,000, half of their expenses.[1] The recent special commission strongly recommends that all the insane poor be cared for in state institutions at the expense of the commonwealth, and it seems probable that the recommendation will soon be adopted.[2]

There are certain apparent advantages in a centralized administration of poor relief. The maximum efficiency at the lowest *per capita* cost can thus be secured. It permits the classification of dependents in accordance with their different needs. The young may be separated from the old, the able-bodied from the infirm, the vicious from the worthy, the sane from the insane. Separate institutions may be constructed to suit the varying needs of these different classes. By this division of labor, also, the best administrative talent and the best methods are universalized. But while centralized administration has its advantages, there is a certain kind of poor relief that cannot advantageously be adapted to it. Temporary relief can best be administered locally. A little temporary relief will often suffice, where removal to a distant state institution would result in permanent pauperization. In the centralized administration of the relief of dependent children and the insane poor, we see the

[1] *Report of the State Board of Lunacy and Charity*, 1897, p. 181.

[2] *Report of the Commission on Charitable and Reformatory Interests*, 1897, p. 23–25.

beginnings of a differentiation between centralized and decentralized poor relief. It seems probable that this differentiation will continue, and the aged poor, the infirm, and other
classes will be cared for in the state institutions, while local
relief will be confined more and more exclusively to relief
of a temporary nature.

Central Administrative Supervision of Local Poor Relief.
Annual reports were first required of local overseers of the
poor in 1837.[1] Up to 1863, when the state board of charities was created these returns were submitted to the secretary
of the commonwealth, who annually compiled an abstract
of them. As a rule, these returns were very incomplete,
some of the towns not responding at all, while the returns of
others were plainly inaccurate. Under the supervision of
the state board, however, they have become much more valuable.

Since 1851 the central board has had charge of auditing
the accounts of the towns for the care of the state poor.
The towns are required to notify the state board of all cases
in which relief is given to state poor.[2] The state board then
sends an agent to investigate the case; to see that it is a
proper case for relief, to investigate the settlement of the
pauper, and to decide whether he shall be relieved by the
town or removed to a state almshouse. The bills presented
by the cities and towns are also carefully investigated, with
the result that the state annually saves a large amount of
money. In 1897 the claims of the towns amounted to
$173,862.36; this amount was reduced by the investigations

[1] Act of April 18, 1837.

[2] The towns, under certain restrictions, may grant aid to the sick state poor
(*Public Statutes*, chap. 86, sec. 25), to those in need of temporary assistance
(*Acts*, 1891, 90), and in cases where the wife has a legal settlement but the hus-
band has not (*Public Statutes*, chap. 86, sec. 31). The state also reimburses the
towns for the burial of state poor (*Public Statutes*, chap. 84, sec. 17).

of the board to $125,107.49, a saving to the state of $48,754.87.[1]

Many towns have no almshouses, their dependents being placed in private families or boarded in the almshouses of other towns. Previous to 1897, it had been the custom of a few towns to auction off their unfortunate poor to the lowest bidder at town meeting. In a few other towns the selectmen placed the poor in the private families offering to care for them at the lowest price. To do away with this reprehensible practice, a law was enacted providing that the state board may determine in what manner overseers of the poor shall make contracts for the support of town paupers, and may visit and inspect all places in which paupers are so supported.[2]

It is the duty of the state board, at least once a year, to visit all neglected and dependent children supported by the cities and towns, and to investigate their condition.[3] When the overseers of the poor of cities and towns fail to comply with the law forbidding the retention in almshouses of pauper children, the authority vested in the overseers may be exercised by the state board to the exclusion of the overseers.

It is the duty of the state board to inspect all places in which insane paupers are kept. As most cities and towns have some mild cases of insanity in their almshouses, practically, this results in the inspection of all local pauper institutions. Where insane persons are found to be improperly cared for, committal to a state asylum may be required. Further than this the board has no compulsory authority Abuses noted by the state visitor are, however, called to the attention of the local authorities, and their correction often follows.

[1] *Report of the State Board of Lunacy and Charity*, 1897, p. 48.

[2] *Acts*, 1897, 374.   [3] *Public Statutes*, chap. 89, sec. 53.

Condensed reports of the state agent on the conditions existing in each city and town pauper institution are published in the annual report of the state board, and the abuses thus brought to the attention of the public and the legislature. Publicity is perhaps the greatest need in regard to local poor relief; and there is at present much room for improvement in that respect. At present there is probably less general knowledge concerning the administration of local poor relief than concerning any other important branch of local administration. Almost every family has its representative in the schools and everyone uses the streets. All are directly interested in good schools and clean streets, and are usually able to detect inefficiency in their administration. They are thus able to hold officials to a strict responsibility. With the almshouse the case is very different. Very few have ever visited it. Only the poor unfortunates who inhabit the almshouse have any personal knowledge concerning its administration. Unless its condition is investigated and reported to the people by some special agency, it is impossible for the people to hold the overseers of the poor and the keeper of the almshouse to a strict account. Publicity is the *sine quâ non* of political responsibility.

It seems probable that in this case the function of investigating and reporting can best be performed by the commonwealth. The agent of the commonwealth, by devoting his entire energy to the work of investigating local almshouses, becomes an expert. By knowing the condition of all the almshouses, the best, as well as the poorest, he is able to judge better the merits and faults of each. His work, moreover, will have the very essential quality of being considered reliable. A local investigation can seldom escape the suspicion of being prejudiced and partial—there is always room for the suspicion that it has been influenced by personal or partisan considerations. The state agent having no personal interest in the conditions or individuals concerned, can be trusted to interpret the facts impartially.

The very unsatisfactory condition of poor relief in the small, declining towns seems also to demand increased central interference. One hundred and thirty-six towns maintain no almshouse; their dependents being placed in private families or boarded in the almshouses of other towns. The number of towns without almshouses is greater than it was in 1864—the year after the establishment of the state board of charities. Then 116 towns were without almshouses; the number has since increased to 136.[1] These are as a rule the smaller towns. Many of them have been declining steadily year after year in population and wealth. It is not to be expected that each will maintain an almshouse for its few dependents, and it is not desirable that it should. The interests of efficiency and economy demand a consolidation of existing almshouses, rather than a further increase of their number. The towns already possess the authority to unite for the purpose of maintaining a common almshouse, though but two such districts have as yet been formed.[2] All the towns now without almshouses might be grouped into districts—in the same manner that they are now being grouped into districts for the purpose of employing school superintendents.[3] If the county in Massachusetts held the same important position that it holds in all other states outside of New England, the problem would more naturally be solved by adopting the plan of county almshouses.

What, then, is the true relation of the commonwealth to public poor relief? In the first place, as in the case of pub-

---

[1] The number of almshouses was but two less in 1897 than in 1864, but the number of cities and towns had increased from 334 to 353. See *Report of the State Board of Lunacy and Charity*, 1897, pp. 103-4.

[2] *Public Statutes*, c. 33, § 5.

[3] See above, p. 28.

lic education, we must recognize that poor relief is a matter
not merely of local but of general concern. As we have
seen, there are classes of dependents that can best be cared
for in state institutions. Here the commonwealth should
have a large sphere of activity entirely independent of the
local authorities; the necessity for a centralized administration is unquestioned. The relation of the commonwealth to
that class of poor relief which from its nature requires to be
locally administered, is a much more difficult problem. We
cannot say, as in the case of the public school, that the interests of the municipality and the commonwealth are substantially identical. A town that maintained no school
would suffer from the fact that its most progressive inhabitants would move to a place where school advantages could
be obtained; but if a town maintains no almshouse, or can
shift the support of its paupers upon others, it may prevent
the coming of undesirable classes and at the same time save
itself a considerable expense. The immense floating population of the present time also greatly complicates the problem. Moreover, the tramp evil can be effectively dealt with
only by concerted action throughout the state. If the local
authorities are to administer poor relief, therefore, they
must be subjected to a strong central control; the entire
system of poor relief throughout the commonwealth must
be organized through a central board.

CHAPTER IV

PENAL INSTITUTIONS

AT first the punishment and confinement of criminals in Massachusetts was attended to either by the town or by the central government. The county did not exist. It was only developed after the expansion of population had, owing to the difficulties of transportation and communication, made it inconvenient to administer some of the functions of the general government from a single center. In this way the maintenance of prisons was gradually shifted from the central government to the counties. It was inconvenient to bring all prisoners to Boston for confinement, for the same reason that it was inconvenient to transact all judicial business from that center. But with improved facilities for transportation, better roads, railroads and inter-municipal electric railways, the present century has witnessed a movement in the opposite direction. County prisons are being superseded by state prisons.

1. *Period of Decentralization.*

The Puritans had comparatively little use for prisons. The stocks, the pillory, and the whipping-post were relied upon for the punishment and correction of minor offenders. These, together with a "cage" for temporary confinement, comprised the penal institutions of the town. More serious offenses were punished by expulsion from the colony, and death was the penalty for a great number of crimes. The prison or house of correction of that time bears a closer resemblance to the town work-house and state farm of the

439]   55 present than to present county houses of correction and state prisons.

In 1632 the general court ordered the first general prison to be built at Boston.[1]   Not until twenty years afterwards did it become necessary to provide for a certain degree of decentralization.   In 1652 the general court ordered that,[2] " Whereas there is only one prison in this jurisdiction, and [it is] very inconvenient to send persons so far remote to the prison at Boston, when there is occasion, it [is] therefore hereby ordered that there shall be another prison erected in this jurisdiction, and that to be at Ipswich ; and there shall be allowed by the country forty pounds for the effecting the same ; and the work to be carried on and managed by the selectmen of the said town."   Nine years afterwards, for the same reasons, it was ordered that Springfield and North-ampton " be allowed their country rate, for this year ensu-ing, for and towards the erecting of a prison or house of cor-rection at Springfield." [3]

With the institution of separate prisons, in the various counties of the colony, their support and management, ex-cept in the case of the prison at Boston, at once became the function of the county courts.   The prison at Boston remained in part a general prison for the whole colony until the changes under the new charter of 1692.   The prison itself and the house for the keeper were originally built by the colony ; and the prison keeper was appointed and paid by the general court.   Soon, however, the appointment of the keeper was transferred to the county of Suffolk, and the ex-pense of repair and reconstruction was divided between the county and the colony.[4]

[1] *Colony Records*, v. 1, p. 100.   [2] *Ibid.*, v. 3, p. 260.

[3] *Ibid.*, v. 4, pt. 2, p. 21.

[4] See *Ibid.*, v. 2, pp. 148, 195; v. 3, pp. 190, 232; v. 4, pt. 2, pp. 120, 137, 575; *Province Laws*, v. 7, pp. 33, 641.

2. *Period of Centralization.*

Establishment of State Prisons. There was no general prison from 1692 to 1785. For the employment and secure confinement of hardened criminals sentenced for long periods or for life, the insecurely constructed county jails became notoriously inadequate. Accordingly, in 1785, Castle Island in the harbor of Boston was made a place for the confinement at hard labor of convicts of the worst class.[1] The experiment was not entirely satisfactory, the island proving no more secure as a place of confinement than the county jails.[2] In 1798 Castle Island was ceded to the national government, and it became necessary to provide some other place for the confinement of convicts.[3] In 1803 it was decided to build a state prison at Charlestown. This was opened in 1805.

About 1820 a considerable interest in the improvement of prison conditions was aroused. With the exception of the long term convicts who were sent to the state prison, the convicted and the unconvicted, male and female, young and old, hardened criminals and those in prison for the first time, men of all conditions and of all degrees of crime, were crowded together in ill-constructed unsanitary prisons with no possibility of a proper classification. The evils of this condition of affairs were enormously increased by the fact that no employment was provided for the prisoners.

To be sure, ever since 1655, the law had continuously provided that in addition to a jail, each county should maintain a house of correction for the employment of convicted prisoners, but during all these years this law had remained a dead letter. First passed in 1655,[4] it was substantially renewed under the province in 1699,[5] under the commonwealth

---

[1] Laws of March 14 and 15, 1785.

[2] Haynes, *Massachusetts State Prison*, pp. 13–14.

[3] Law of June 25, 1798.   [4] *Colony Records*, v. 3, pp. 375, 399.

[5] *Province Laws* , v. 1, p. 378.

in 1788,[1] and again in 1834.[2]   The first house of correction, properly so-called, was opened in Boston in 1823,[3] and for a long time it was the model institution of the kind in the state.

Boston also led the way in the establishment of a reformatory for juvenile offenders.[4]   Although the promoters of this reform recognized that such a reformatory should properly be established for the benefit of the entire state, they saw no prospect that the state would undertake the project. The need for such an institution was naturally more intense in a city than in the rural districts.   Had Boston been compelled to await state initiative for relief in this matter, prison reform would have been delayed many years.

The establishment and successful operation of a reformatory for juvenile offenders in Boston, led to the desire, on the part of the other cities and towns of the state, to secure the benefits of such an institution for themselves.   The state as a whole became interested in the matter, and, as a result, a state reform school for boys was established at Westborough in 1846, and a similar institution for girls at Lancaster in 1854.

In 1869 it was provided that vagrants and drunkards might be sentenced to the state farm at Bridgewater instead of to the town workhouse or county house of correction. Since 1819 the state prison had been used exclusively for male convicts, and female convicts were imprisoned in the county jails and houses of correction.   The establishment of a reformatory prison for women in 1874 greatly relieved the county prisons, and made a better classification possible; a movement which was also greatly furthered by the establishment of the Massachusetts Reformatory in 1884, for the re-

---

[1] Law of March 26, 1788.   [2] *Acts*, 1834, 151.

[3] Quincy, *Municipal History of Boston*, pp. 102–105; *Second Report of the State Board of Charities*, pp. 22–31.

Established in 1826.   Quincy, *op. cit.*, pp. 106–109.

ception of the younger male prisoners sentenced for a year or more.

Central Administrative Control. But aside from this direct assumption on the part of the state of much of the work formerly left to the counties, a very considerable central administrative control over county prisons has gradually been developed. This control first took the form of requiring annual reports from the local authorities. As early as 1834 [1] a law was passed requiring county commissioners to make annual returns to the secretary of the commonwealth in regard to jails and houses of correction. But as no penalty was provided for failure to make returns, the law, though compulsory in form, as a matter of fact had only the effect of a formal request, which local officials might comply with or ignore, as they saw fit. In 1856 the secretary explains the situation as follows: "Notwithstanding the law is explicit in requiring of the sheriffs and overseers of the houses of correction true answers to the inquiries contained in the blanks aforesaid, in some cases these officers seem to have regarded it as a matter wholly within their own choice whether to answer or not, while in others the answers are so imperfect and confused as to be entitled to little or no credit." [2] Accordingly in the following year a heavy penalty was provided for failure to make returns, and since that time, under the direction successively of the secretary of state, the state board of charities and the prison commission, these returns have been quite satisfactory.

In 1833 a special commission was appointed to make a personal inspection of all jails and houses of correction. Some years afterwards it became customary for the joint standing committee on prisons, on the authorization of the

[1] *Acts*, 1834, 151.

[2] See *Secretary of State's Abstract of the Returns of Keepers of Jails and Overseers of Houses of Correction,* 1856.

legislature, to make an annual investigation of all county prisons. This committee, in 1848, reports as follows:[1] "The prisoners are crowded together from the fact that many of the rooms are not trustworthy, and often because they cannot be warmed, and the convicted and the unconvicted, the young and old, are mixed up with an indiscrimination entirely in violation of law." But usually the investigations of these legislative committees were without result. As is usual in the case of such committees, they had a pleasant trip at the state's expense, were received and feasted as the guests of the prison keepers, and naturally came back with nothing in particular to report.

In 1863 the state board of charities was created. Among its duties was that of making an annual investigation of all places in which insane persons were confined. As jails and houses of correction were often used for this purpose, they were now subjected to an annual inspection, but this was the extent of the powers of the board.

In 1870, in spite of the assurance of the committee of the legislature of the preceding year that "they found the correctional institutions of the commonwealth generally in a satisfactory condition,"[2] there were a considerable number of individuals who were convinced that the county prisons were not all that they should be, and who succeeded in inducing the legislature to establish a board of prison commissioners.[3] The board as at present organized consists of five unsalaried members appointed by the governor and council for terms of five years. Two of the five members must be women. The term of one member expires annually. The board appoints a paid secretary to act as its executive officer.[4] The board is given an extensive control over county prisons. Among its powers and duties are the following:

[1] *House Documents*, 1848, no. 208.   [2] *Senate Documents*, 1869, no. 392.
[3] *Acts*, 1870, 370.   [4] *Acts*, 1879, 294.

1. The classification of all prisoners with reference to sex, age, character, condition and offense. In order to accomplish this it may remove prisoners from the jail or house of correction in which they are confined, to any jail or house of correction in the state; and it may remove any female prisoner to the state reformatory for women.

2. The preparation of rules, with the approval of the governor and council, for the direction of prison officials, the government of convicts, and the custody and preservation of prison property.

3. The approval of all plans for the construction or enlargement of county prisons.[1]

4. The inspection of all county prisons at least every six months.

5. The preparation of an annual report to the legislature concerning the condition of county prisons, with such recommendations and suggestions as it may deem proper.

In 1887, for the purpose of regulating prison labor, the office of general superintendent of prisons was created.[2] He is a salaried official, appointed by the governor with the consent of the council, and holding office at the pleasure of the governor. He is not under the control of the state board of commissioners of prisons. He is given an extensive control over the prison industries of jails and houses of correction, as well as of the state prisons. Among his powers over county prisons are the following:

1. He may make rules and regulations for the purchase of tools, machinery, and raw materials, and for the sale of the manufactured products.

2. His approval is necessary in regard to the number, compensation, appointment and removal of trade instructors; to the compensation and appointment of purchasing and

---

[1] *Acts*, 1897, 316.   [2] *Ibid.*, 1887, 447.

selling agents; and he must approve all salary rolls and all accounts contracted in purchase of tools, machinery and materials.

A very extensive control is thus seen to be given to the commissioners of prisons and to the general superintendent of prisons. Its exercise has been very beneficial in improving the condition of the county prisons, and in systematizing the entire prison administration of the state. But it has been found impossible to secure the proper classification and employment of prisoners under the county system. There are fourteen counties in the state, and each, with the exception of Dukes, is required to maintain a separate jail and house of correction. In almost half of these counties, the average number of convicts is so small that their proper classification and employment can be obtained only at so great an expense that it is practically out of the question. The expense per convict of an efficient prison management decreases up to a certain point with the number of convicts. The county system is uneconomical and inefficient. The county is not at all adapted to use as a district for prison administration. In order to secure the best results, the smaller houses of correction should be consolidated, and each should be devoted to a special class of prisoners. In order to accomplish this, it has been proposed that the commonwealth assume entire control and management of the county houses of correction, and that the state be divided into such a number of prison districts as will secure the organization of the entire prison system on the most effective and economical basis.[1]

Modern ideas concerning the treatment and reform of criminals can be realized only by a high degree of specialization and centralization. Special institutions, specially con-

[1] Report of the commissioners of prisons on the division of the state into prison districts, *Senate Documents*, 1877, no. 4.

structed and equipped, with skilled penologists in charge, must be provided for the various grades and conditions of criminals. This can only be secured (except at an expense that renders it practically impossible) by the centralization of the entire penal administration.[1]

[1] "Old and poorly arranged buildings, the imprisonment of both sexes in the same prison, and in some cases in the same wing of a prison, the congregating together in the same prison of persons from every condition in life and experience in crime, form some of the objections to the present arrangement of county control of the different jails and houses of correction.

"There is at present an average of about 800 women in the county prisons in the State. Under a single management, one or two of the existing houses of correction could be utilized for prisons for women, others for the imprisonment of minor offenders which come under the class known as misdemeanors, while other prisons could be easily arranged for the retention of a class known to have a longer experience in crime." *Prison Commissioners' Report*, 1897, p. 270.

CHAPTER V—PUBLIC HEALTH

I. PUBLIC HEALTH

a. *Period of Decentralization*

FOR a considerable period of time after the settlement of Massachusetts Bay, each of the several towns took care of its health interests in its own way. No general law was passed on the subject of contagious diseases until 1702, yet each town previous to this time took such measures as it deemed necessary to prevent the spread of disease.

In 1647 a plague in the Barbadoes led to the passage of the first quarantine law. It provides for the quarantine of all vessels from the West Indies, under the direction of the council or a committee of the council.[1] This quarantine was in effect about two years. Again, in 1665 a temporary quartine was established on account of the great plague in London. Vessels from England could land their passengers and cargoes only on receiving permission from the governor or the general court.[2]

A general act for preventing the spread of contagious diseases was first passed in 1702.[3] In regard to infected vessels, the act provides that any justice of the peace may take the necessary temporary measures. He must give notice of his action to the governor, who, with the advice and consent of the council, may issue such further orders as may be deemed necessary. The selectmen of towns are given power to iso-

---

[1] *Colony Records*, v. 2, p. 237.   [2] *Ibid.*, v. 4, pt. 2, p. 280.
[3] *Province Laws*, v. 1, p. 469.

late all persons within their borders falling sick with contagious diseases.   This law was the direct result of a severe
outbreak of small-pox in Boston, by which 4.4 per cent. of
the population died.   Though amended from time to time,
it continued in force until 1797.

In 1716 a quarantine station was established by the province on Spectacle Island.[1]   The station was placed under
the direct supervison of the selectmen of Boston, who were
to furnish the necessary accommodations and contract with
the keeper at the expense of the province.[2]

Up to 1739 no measures had been taken to prevent infected persons from coming into the province by land from
the neighboring colonies.   It was now provided that the
selectmen of any border town might station persons at the
main places of entrance from the other colonies, in order to
examine travelers and to prevent infected persons from entering.[3]

The power given to the governor and council by the law
of 1702 to issue orders regarding the quarantine of vessels
became gradually less and less in successive laws, and finally
disappeared in 1797.

Previous to 1797 there was no provision for local boards
of health.   The abatement of public nuisances as well as the
prevention of contagious diseases were in the hands of the
justices of the peace and the selectmen of the town.   Proceedings for the removal of nuisances were usually made on
the complaint of some individual whose interests were being
injured by the nuisance complained of.   The law of 1797
leaves the powers relating to quarantine and contagious diseases with the selectmen, but permits any town to create a

[1] *Province Laws*, v. 2, p. 65.

[2] *Ibid.*, v. 2, p. 91.   See also *Acts Relating to the Establishment of Quarantine*,
Boston Board of Health, 1881.

[3] *Province Laws*, v. 2, p. 988.

board of health or health officer to have charge of the removal of nuisances. Little use, however, was made by the towns of the powers thus granted. The small towns did not see fit to provide a special board for the abatement of public nuisances and the needs of the more populous towns required boards with more extensive powers.

The first board of health was created in Boston in 1799 by a special act of the legislature.[1] The law was the result of a severe epidemic of yellow fever during the previous year. The board was composed of members elected by the people, and in it were consolidated all the powers formerly exercised by the selectmen in relation to the administration of the quarantine laws, the prevention of contagious diseases, and the abatement of public nuisances. Modeled upon this law other special acts were passed for several of the larger towns. When these towns became incorporated as cities the powers vested in the health board were vested in the city council, to be exercised by the council or delegated to a separate board, as it might determine. In Boston the health powers of the council were delegated to the mayor and aldermen. In most of the cities the city marshal was given the supervision of all matters relating to the public health. But few of the towns chose special boards of health; the selectmen acting in that capacity.[2] In Boston the matter was well supervised and considerable systematic work was done, but in many of the towns no thought was apparently given to the subject, and in others only spasmodic efforts were made.

b. Period of Centralization.

Such was the condition in 1849, when the Asiatic cholera invaded the state. Seven hundred and seven died from its effects in Boston alone. This led to an awakening. A

---

[1] Laws of February 13 and June 29, 1799.

[2] See *Report of the Sanitary Commission of Massachusetts*, 1850.

state commission was appointed to prepare a plan for a sanitary survey of the state. The commission, in its very able report, recommended, among other things, that each town be required to appoint a board of health, and that a state board be established. This board was " to have the general direction of each census; to superintend the execution of the sanitary laws of the state; to examine and decide upon sanitary questions submitted to it by public authorities; to advise the state as to the sanitary arrangements of public buildings and public institutions; to give instructions to local boards of health as to their powers and duties; to suggest local sanitary rules and regulations; to recommend such measures as they may deem expedient for the prevention of diseases and the promotion of the public health; and to report their proceedings annually to the state."[1] Many of these recommendations have since been carried out, but a beginning even was not made until about twenty years afterwards. In 1861 a memorial to the legislature of the Boston sanitary association respectfully represents " that the interests of human health and life . . . require more of the paternal care, watchfulness and protection of the legislature than they now receive, and these objects may be best attained by the establishment of a state board of health."[2]

The demand for some control over the town health authorities is evidenced in the law of 1866, providing that any person aggrieved by the neglect or refusal of the town board to abate a nuisance may appeal to the county commissioners, who may hear the appeal and may exercise all the powers in the abatement of the nuisance that the board of health is authorized to exercise.[3] At length, in 1869, a

[1] See *Report of the Sanitary Commission of Massachusetts*, 1850, p. 111.

[2] *House Documents*, 1861, no. 112, p. 1.

[3] *Acts*, 1866, 211.

state board of health was established.[1]   As then organized,
it had no compulsory authority.   Its duty was simply to
make sanitary investigations and to diffuse the information
thus gathered among the people.   Its function was one of
enlightenment, and although it has since been vested with
numerous and important powers, none has proved more
potent.

In 1871 the board was given power to prohibit offensive
trades; in 1878 it was given general supervision of water
supplies.   In 1879 the duties of the board were transferred
to the board of health, lunacy and charity, and this new
board was given co-ordinate powers with the local boards of
health in the prevention of the spread of contagious diseases.
In 1882 the board was given authority to enforce a law
passed to prevent the adulteration of food and drugs.   In
1885 a separate board of health was created with increased
powers, especially in relation to water supplies and sewerage.
In 1894 all vaccine institutions were placed under its supervision, and the boards of health of all cities and towns of
over five thousand inhabitants were required to send annual
reports of deaths to the board according to the forms prescribed by it.   These are but the more important steps in its
development; its present organization and powers will now
be more fully considered.

The state board of health consists of seven persons appointed by the governor, with the consent of the council.
Their term of office is seven years, so arranged that the term
of one member expires annually.   The board appoints a
secretary, who acts as its executive officer.

1. *General powers of the board*.   It is the duty of the
board to take cognizance of the general interests of health
throughout the commonwealth; to make investigations concerning the causes of disease and epidemics, and the influence

[1] *Acts*, 1869, 420.

of locality, employment and condition upon health, and to
diffuse information in regard to these things among the
people.[1]

2. *Clothing made in unhealthy workshops.*   Upon notifica-
tion from the chief of the district police, it is the duty of the
board to examine workshops in which clothing is made, and
issue the necessary orders to protect the public health.   It
also has power to protect the public from clothing made in
unhealthy workshops outside of the state.[2]

3. *Offensive trades.*   Upon complaint, and after notice and
hearing, the board may order the discontinuance of any
noxious or offensive trade or occupation in the place where
it is at the time established.   The location and plans of construction of all crematories,[3] and of all swine slaughtering
establishments,[4] are subject to the approval of the board, and
it may establish regulations for their government.   Cities
and towns must first secure its approval for taking or purchasing land for the purification and disposal of sewage.[5]

4. *Food and drug inspection.*   The board appoints inspectors and chemists, and takes the necessary measures to
enforce the laws of the state relating to the adulteration of
foods and drugs.   It may expend eleven thousand dollars
annually for this purpose, but not less than three-fifths of
this amount must be expended for the enforcement of the
laws against the adulteration of milk and milk products.[6]

5. *Impure ice.*   Upon the complaint of twenty-five consumers of ice cut from any pond or stream in the commonwealth, the board, after notice, may give a hearing to determine whether the ice is impure and injurious to health.   If
found to be injurious, the board may forbid its sale.[7]

[1] *Acts*, 1888, 101.   [2] *Ibid.*, 1891, 357; 1892, 296.
[3] *Ibid.*, 1885, 265.   [4] *Public Statutes*, c. 107, §§ 2, 4, 5.
[5] *Acts*, 1890, 124.   [6] *Ibid.*, 1882, 263; 1884, 289; 1891, 412.
[7] *Ibid.*, 1886, 287.

6. *Water supplies and sewerage.* The board has the general oversight and care of all inland waters. It examines them to see whether they are adapted for use as sources of water supply or are in a condition likely to impair the public health. It recommends suitable plans for systems of main sewers and such other measures as it deems necessary for preventing the pollution of water supplies. It may conduct experiments to determine the best methods for the purification and disposal of sewage.[1]

The board has authority to make rules, regulations and orders for preventing the pollution of streams or ponds used as a source of water supply by any city or town, or any water or ice company. Upon the complaint of the authorities of any city or town or the president of a water or ice company, that the source of supply is being polluted by individuals, the board, after giving notice and hearing, may order them to desist.[2]

The board consults with and advises cities, towns, corporations, firms and individuals concerning the best source of water supply and the best practicable method of disposing of their sewage; and all such municipalities, associations and individuals must submit to the board for its advice plans of their proposed schemes in relation to water supply and sewage; and all petitions to the legislature for authority to introduce a system of water supply or sewage must be accompanied by the recommendations of the board thereon. It is the duty of the board to report to the attorney-general all cases of failure to comply with the laws relating to the pollution of inland waters.[3]

7. *Infectious and contagious diseases.* Local boards of health are required to notify the state board within twenty-four hours after obtaining knowledge of a case of a con-

---

[1] *Acts*, 1888, 375.   [2] *Ibid.*, 1897, 510.   [3] *Ibid.*, 1888, 375.

tagious or infectious disease.[1]   Upon receipt of information
that such a disease exists or is likely to exist in any locality,
the board investigates the matter and consults with the local
authorities concerning the best means of preventing the
spread of the disease; and it may exercise powers coördi-
nate with those of the local board of health.[2]   The board
has established a plant for the production of antitoxin,
for distribution to local boards, hospitals and physicians.
It also examines the products of certain diseases sent to it
by local boards and physicians for the purpose of determin-
ing the disease, notably diphtheria, tuberculosis and malarial
fever.

8. *Reports of local boards.*   Local boards of health in cities
and towns of more than five thousand inhabitants are required to make annual reports of deaths to the state board,
and according to the forms prescribed by it.[3]

The most important work of the state board has probably
been in relation to its control over water supplies and sewerage.   Eastern Massachusetts is so thickly dotted with populous cities and towns that central supervision has been absolutely necessary to prevent the streams from being turned
into noisome sewers and to protect the water supplies from
pollution.   When individuals come together in cities a common system of sewerage and water supply becomes necessary; and when cities and villages are themselves so
closely crowded together as they are in that territory
lying within about thirty miles of the state house at Boston,
the problem of water supply and sewerage can no longer be
left to each individual municipality.   It then becomes necessary to provide common water supplies and common main
sewers for a number of cities and towns.   In this connection
the state board has rendered valuable service.   At the re-

[1] *Acts*, 1893, 302.   [2] *Ibid.*, 1894, 218.   [3] *Ibid.*

quest of the legislature it has made careful surveys and prepared elaborate plans for systems of sewers and water supply for extensive districts, and its plans have usually been
carried out.

The work of the board in giving advice to local authorities,
companies and individuals is extensive and is constantly increasing. Upon request, the experts in the employ of the
board examine existing or proposed water supplies, make a
careful analysis of the water and report the results. Plans
for sewage disposal are also carefully considered. A systematic examination of the water supplies of the state was
begun in 1887 and the work has since been continued.[1]

We see, therefore, that although the state board possesses

[1] The death rate in Massachusetts has remained practically stationary during
the past forty years in spite of the fact that the average density of population has
doubled. Improved sanitary conditions have very nearly counterbalanced the
unfavorable influence of increasing density. "Infectious diseases generally, including consumption, have diminished, while most of the so-called local diseases
(those of the nervous, respiratory, circulatory organs, etc.), have increased, and
the result has been a balance or a maintenance of uniformity in the general
death-rate." See *Report of the State Board of Health*, 1896, pp. 711–829. The
work of the state board, especially in the matter of water supplies and sewerage, has doubtless had a very great influence in bringing abont the decline in
deaths from infectious diseases.

Five-year period.	Number of persons per square mile.	Death-rate per 1,000 caused by pneumonia, kidney diseases, heart disease, brain diseases, and cancer.	Death-rate per 1,000 caused by small-pox, measles, scarlet fever, diphtheria, croup, typhoid fever, cholera infantum, consumption, whooping cough, dysentery, and child-birth.	Aggregate death-rate per 1,000 persons.
1856–60	144.4	2.77	8.17	17.94
1861–65	150.6	3.47	9.30	20.71
1866–70	165.8	3.66	7.48	18.19
1871–75	189.0	4.49	8.49	20.83
1876–80	208.0	4.68	7.31	18.84
1881–85	225.7	5.67	6.51	19.82
1886–90	254.5	6.22	5.68	19.41
1891–95	287.8	6.88	5.05	19.83

great powers, it can exercise little direct control over the local authorities. Its chief coercive powers are exercised upon the individual directly. In many cases its powers are simply co-ordinate with those of the local boards; either may act, but in case one acts there is no necessity for action on the part of the other. This is largely the case with reference to food and drug inspection, offensive trades, and contagious diseases. Municipalities, like other corporations and firms, must submit the plans of proposed water supply and sewerage systems to the state board for its advice, but are not compelled to follow the advice given. They must also make reports of deaths and contagious diseases to the state board; the requirement of reports is, however, one of the weakest forms of administrative control.

While the powers of the state board have been enormously increased, it has not been at the expense of the importance of the local boards. The work of the state board has resulted in increased local activity; separate boards of health have been established where none previously existed, and inactive boards have become more efficient. The state board reports that owing to the increased activity of the local boards, its interference in the matter of offensive trades is now seldom called for. A state association of boards of health has been formed for the discussion of matters pertaining to health administration. As the density of population increases, additional powers and duties are being constantly imposed upon the local boards.

There can be no question but that the maintenance of sanitary conditions in any part of the commonwealth is of vital importance to every other part of the commonwealth, but it does not follow from this that the public health administration should be completely centralized. The self-interest of the municipality can in the main be relied upon to lead it to take the necessary sanitary measures. The interests of the municipality and the commonwealth are substantially identical. There are, however, as we have seen, certain functions which must be exercised by an authority of broader jurisdiction than the municipality, and others that must be centrally administered in the interests of economy and efficiency. Aside from these, one of the most important duties of a state board should be that of educating municipalities as to what are their real interests. In case, however, the municipality neglects to act, the commonwealth must act for its own defense. Such action may take the form either of compelling the local officials to perform their duty, or of its independent performance by central officials. In case, however, it is necessary to exercise coercive authority over the individual, it is much simpler for the state board to exercise that authority directly than to coerce an unwilling local board into coercing the individual. This upon the whole represents the actual relation of the commonwealth to the public health in Massachusetts. There has been a considerable differentiation between the municipalities and the commonwealth in the work of health administration.

II. VITAL STATISTICS.

A little more than a decade after the settlement of Salem, the general court passed its first law for the collection of vital statistics. September 9, 1639, Mr. Steven Winthrope was chosen "to record things," and it was ordered that records of births, deaths and marriages be kept in every town, and that they be brought annually to the colony recorder, to be entered upon his books.[1] Three years later, the annual return was required to be made to the district court instead of to the colony recorder.[2] When the law came to be re-enacted under the province in 1692, the town clerk, though

---

[1] *Colony Records*, v. 1, p. 276.   [2] *Ibid.*, v. 2, p. 15.

still required to keep a record of births, deaths and marriages, was required to make no report either to the county court or to the province recorder. Central control, strong at the start, had been weakened in 1642, and was now practically abolished. Some towns may have kept up their records, but it is not probable that many did·so. The law, though a dead letter, was kept in the statute books for one hundred and fifty years. Then in 1842 a return was made to the system with which the state started out in 1639. The clerks of cities and towns were required to make annual returns to the secretary of the commonwealth according to the forms prepared by him. The secretary was also authorized to issue instructions and explanations to aid the clerks in making their returns. For a number of years it was very difficult to get some of the clerks into the habit of making these reports, and most of those made were very imperfect. By increased penalties and patient supervision on the part of the secretary of state, however, their accuracy and value has been greatly increased, and they have become much more detailed.

III. STATE BOARD OF CATTLE COMMISSIONERS.

Previous to 1860 no provision had been made for either state or local action for the prevention of contagious diseases among domestic animals. In 1859 pleuro-pneumonia made its appearance in several cattle herds of the state. The disease spread rapidly, and the knowledge of the disastrous effects attending its spread in other countries, led to decisive action. The mayor and aldermen of cities and the selectmen of towns were given summary powers to take the necessary measures to stamp out the disease, and a state cattle commission was established with even more broad and summary powers.[1] The regulations of the state board super-

[1] *Acts*, 1860, 192, 221.

seded those of the local authorities, and the local authorities were required to carry out all orders and directions given them by the central board. As a result of these drastic measures, the commission, though its work had been completely blocked during one year by an insufficient appropriation, was in 1866 able to report the complete extirpation of the disease. In 1868 the commission took effective measures to prevent the introduction of Texas fever. Two years later a new disease known as the "foot and mouth" disease appeared, and through the vigorous measures of the commission it was suppressed in 1872. In 1874 and 1875 there was a slight outbreak of Texas fever. This led to the passage of a law in 1876, forbidding the importation of Texas cattle between May and November of each year, and making it the duty of the cattle commission to enforce the law. In 1878 the commission and the local authorities were given the same power in relation to contagious diseases among all other domestic animals that they previously had in relation to cattle. In 1881, the United States supreme court having decided in a Missouri case that a law forbidding the transportation of Texas cattle through or into a state was unconstitutional, the legislature authorized the cattle commission to quarantine all Texas cattle coming into the state.

Alarmed at the spread of tuberculosis among cattle, and the great danger to human life resulting, the legislature in 1892 took measures to check it. In 1876 an act had been passed permitting any city or town to appoint one or more inspectors of provisions and of animals intended for slaughter or kept for the production of milk. Many cities and a few towns had taken advantage of it. Now, however, the appointment of inspectors was made obligatory, and the inspectors were required to report to the state commission all cases of tuberculosis coming to their notice. No penalty was attached for failure to comply, however, and notwithstanding the frequent orders of the commission, during the first year four towns failed to appoint inspectors, and the inspectors of 235 of the 351 cities and towns in the state made no report to the commission. This failure, and the belief that concerted, systematic action was absolutely necessary to stamp out the dread disease, led in the next two years to an almost complete subjection of the local authorities to the control and direction of the central commission. The present organization and powers of the commission will now be briefly considered.[1]

The state board of cattle commissioners consists of five members, appointed by the governor with the consent of the council. Their term of office is three years, unless sooner removed by the appointing power, and the commissions of the entire board may be terminated by the governor and council when in their judgment the public safety permits.

The commission has power to make regulations concerning the prevention and suppression of contagious diseases among domestic animals and the treatment and destruction of animals that have been exposed to or are affected with any contagious disease. Such orders and regulations supersede those of the local boards of health. Local boards of health and inspectors of provisions must carry out and enforce all lawful regulations and directions of the commission, under penalty of not exceeding five hundred dollars. The commission is authorized to appoint agents with equal powers to those conferred by law upon the local inspectors, and each member of the commission has the same power throughout the commonwealth to inspect and quarantine cattle that is conferred upon local boards of health and inspectors.

Each city and town is required to appoint one or more in-

[1] *Acts*, 1885, 378.

spectors of provisions and animals under penalty of not exceeding five hundred dollars. In case of refusal or neglect to appoint, the commission may do so. In case of neglect or refusal to be sworn or properly to perform the duties of the office, any inspector may be removed by the commission and another appointed to serve the remainder of the term. The commission may fix the compensation of inspectors thus appointed by it, at not exceeding five hundred dollars a year, to be paid by the city or town. Local inspectors are required to make inspections at the times and in the manner prescribed by the commission; the forms of their records are prescribed in detail by the commission, and they are required to make numerous reports to it. The local inspectors are also subject to the direction of the local boards of health, but in case of conflicting directions the orders of the state commission are to be followed.

When an animal suspected of being afflicted with a contagious disease is quarantined by a local inspector, the commission is notified; an agent of the commission makes an examination, and the animal is killed if found to be diseased. The commission takes immediate charge of the examination of all cattle coming into the public markets at Brighton, Watertown and Somerville from without the state, that are not certified to have passed the tuberculin test before entering the state. Arrangements have been entered into with the cattle commissioners of adjoining states whereby nearly all the cattle coming into these markets have been tested by approved veterinarians before entering the state. Except on the written permit of the commission, all cattle brought into the state must be taken to one of these public markets. And all cattle entering under permits are examined by special agents of the commission. The work of the United States bureau of animal industry, established in 1884, has materially aided the commission in its efforts to prevent the introduction of contagious diseases.

The commission, through its special agents, also undertakes the examination of stables and dairies, with a view to securing better sanitary conditions, and thus of protecting the milk consumer from the dangers of impure milk. Only a beginning has yet been made, however, as the power of the commission is limited to that of examination simply. The results of its investigations show conclusively that milk inspection in order to be of great sanitary value must begin at the source of the milk supply; this in the case of Boston consists of thousands of small dairies situated chiefly in eastern Massachusetts and southern New Hampshire, but Maine, Vermont and Connecticut are also drawn upon.[1] It thus becomes an inter-state problem; one with which a New England government might most effectively deal.

The intent of the statute under which the cattle commission was created was the suppression of contagious diseases in the interest of the animal owner, rather than the protection of the consumer against the use of unwholesome animal products. With the fight against tuberculosis the aim has come to be the protection both of the interests of the producer and of the health of the consumer.

The cattle commission presents a most thoroughgoing example of central administrative control over local authorities. The commission may direct, remove, and in certain cases appoint the local inspectors. So far, the power of removal has been exercised but once. It has been the policy of the commission to exercise this power only on rare occasions when there is positive evidence of dishonesty or incompetency. Aside from this, however, the commission has a large sphere in which it acts through its own agents independently of local officials.[2]

[1] See Whitaker, *Milk Supply of Massachusetts Cities.*

[2] Chapter 491 of the act of 1894 is a codification of the laws relating to contagious diseases among domestic animals. It has been amended by chapters 476 and 496 of the act of 1895.

CHAPTER VI

POLICE

I. *The State Police.*

THE present state police force owes its origin to an attempt to prohibit the sale of intoxicating liquors. A statute prohibiting the sale of intoxicants throughout the state was passed in 1852. Previous to this, through local option, the liquor traffic was prohibited throughout a large portion of the state. In 1847 the mayor and aldermen of Boston refused to grant licenses for the sale of liquor, and none were again granted until 1852. This attempt at prohibition in Boston failed; the city marshal in 1851 reported that there were then fifteen hundred places in which liquor was sold.[1] But when Boston, after a five years' trial, at length became convinced that it could not enforce a prohibitory law, the legislature intervened to make prohibition obligatory.

The law of 1852 was very generally enforced in the rural communities, and in many of the smaller urban centers where the local sentiment was strong in its favor, But in Boston, and a few other manufacturing cities having a large foreign population, all pretension of enforcement gradually ceased. The execution of the law being left entirely to the local authorities, it naturally followed that the law was enforced in those cities and towns in which there was a strong local sentiment in its favor and ignored in the others; the law, though compulsory in form, was optional in fact. To be-

---

[1] Winsor, *Memorial History of Boston*, v. 3, p. 253.

lievers in state prohibition, this condition could not be satisfactory; the purpose of the friends of the law had been to make use of the compulsory power of the state to impose prohibition upon unwilling communities. They soon came to a realization of the fact that all that they had secured was the promulgation of the law, and that it was far from being self-executing. It is impossible to exercise coercion by putting the coercive power in the hands of those that are to be coerced.

The demand was, therefore, made for some form of central administration of the law. The most ardent friends of the law favored a system of metropolitan police, by which the police of the large cities, in which the law was being disregarded, would be placed under boards appointed by the governor. A beginning was to be made with Boston and its suburban cities. In 1865 a bill passed the senate constituting Boston, Chelsea, Cambridge, Charlestown and Roxbury a metropolitan police district. It is interesting to note the deep-seated distrust with which the promoters of this measure looked upon large cities. A joint special committee of the legislature reports as follows:[1] " It is necessary to adopt the metropolitan principle in order to prevent the elements which are destructive of property and laws from keeping practical control of the city, and so, from the size and wealth of Boston, and the intimacy of its relations with the whole state, undermining the prosperity and peace of the commonwealth. * * * Moreover, large classes, having the right of citizens, but not the welfare of government at heart, always run into large cities as the common sewers of the state, and are ready to make use of just such machinery as the present system affords to them, to make the material, moral and legal interests of society and the

[1] *Senate Documents*, 1863, no. 129, p. 4.

state subservient to their passion and their will." The
following is taken from the address of the state temper-
ance alliance to the people of Massachusetts in 1864:
" It is never safe for any state to entrust the execution
of its laws to a great city. The larger the city, the greater
the danger. There are frequent and grave issues between
great cities and the laws of the state. In such cases the
laws can never prevail, unless the state controls the police
that executes them."

The city council of Boston on the other hand entered a
vigorous remonstrance against this proposed usurpation of
the city's ancient rights, arguing as follows:[1] "That as general laws administered in local communities by officers of
their own selection has been ever an essential principle of
our free institutions, in our judgment the police powers
should be left as at present to the control of the towns and
cities; and, inasmuch as delegation to independent boards
without responsibility involves expenditure without check
and often the oppressive exercise of power, its charge should
be left to the municipal authorities, who assess the taxes,
are accountable for their economical application, are open to
scrutiny, and liable to be removed by those who have elected
them."

As a compromise between those who desired the metropolitan police plan and the less radical supporters of prohibition, an act to establish a state police was passed in 1865.[2]
As then established the state police consisted of a constable
of the commonwealth appointed and removable by the governor and council and at least twenty deputies for Suffolk
county and one for every other county. The governor and
council could direct the employment of additional deputies.
The constable and his deputies had all the powers of local

[1] *Senate Documents,* 1863, no. 163.

[2] *Acts,* 1865, 249.

police and constables, except the service of civil process, and their jurisdiction extended throughout the commonwealth. It was their duty to see that all the laws of the commonwealth were enforced; and they were charged especially with the suppression of houses of prostitution, gambling places and liquor shops. The constable was subject to the direction of the governor in the execution of the laws and the preservation of the peace. The governor, moreover, was given the power in any emergency, of which he was to be the judge, to assume command of the whole or a part of the municipal police force of any place, and to authorize the constable of the commonwealth to command its assistance in the execution of criminal process, the suppression of riots, and the preservation of the peace.

We see, therefore, that in the establishment of a state police, regard was had not only for the immediate object to be attained, but for the general principles involved. The legislature had come to the conclusion that its general police regulations should no longer be subject to the veto of the local administrative authorities. A force was placed under the direction of the chief executive of the state to enable him to uphold the laws and maintain peace, order and security throughout the commonwealth.

For the special task for which it was established, the suppression of the liquor traffic in the large cities, the state police force proved unequal. A system of metropolitan police might perhaps have been more successful. The few state officers assigned to the city of Boston could not accomplish that which would have been an extremely difficult task for the entire police force of the city. During 1866 the average strength of the force was fifty-eight, and in 1867, eighty-seven. In 1867 it secured 5,331 prosecutions for violation of the liquor law, and made 1,979 liquor seizures.[1]

[1] *Report of the Constable of the Commonwealth*, 1867.

In the following year the prohibitory law was repealed, but after a year's trial of license it was again enacted. In 1871 the force was reorganized.[1] Three police commissioners were appointed, with power to appoint and have general supervision and direction of a chief constable and not exceeding seventy deputy constables. In the following year the police commissioners were authorized to increase the force to one hundred men. In 1874 the powers of the police commissioners were vested in the chief constable.[2] The efforts of the state police to enforce the prohibitory law were unabated, and in 1874 it made 5,912 liquor seizures and secured 7,126 prosecutions.[3] But the apparent impossibility of the task led to the repeal of the prohibitory law in the following year, and to a return to the system of license and local option.

Though reorganized in 1875, the state police force was not abolished. The special service which was the occasion of its establishment, was no longer needed, but during the ten years that it had existed, its services under the general powers granted it had proved so beneficial that it had earned the right to a permanent place in the administrative system of the commonwealth. In 1866 three members were assigned specially to detective duty. Their services proved particularly valuable in detecting thieves at camp-meetings, military musters, and agricultural fairs. While the state constable instructed his deputies to give especial attention to offenses against liquor selling, gambling and prostitution, they were also directed to give attention to complaints against parties charged with violating any criminal statute. When in 1867 a new law was enacted regulating the employment of children in factories, the constable was charged with its execution, and he was required to detail one of his deputies specially for this service.[4]

[1] *Acts*, 1871, 394.
[3] *Acts*, 1874, 405.
[3] *Report of the Chief Constable*, 1874.
[4] *Acts*, 1867, 285.

When the prohibitory law was temporarily repealed, in 1868, a bill passed the legislature to abolish the state police, but was vetoed by the governor. In his veto message one of the chief reasons urged by the governor for the retention of the force was that it was necessary in order to check the increasing demoralization in the larger cities. He was convinced that cities could not be trusted to enforce the numerous laws of the state, passed in the interest of public morality. Upon this point he says: "A prosperous commerce, progress in the arts, and the increase of manufactures have condensed our population in large towns and cities, intensified vicious inclinations, and multiplied the actual number of crimes. This is apparently the price of public prosperity and wealth. Official records display to the public gaze an alarming increase of offenses against the person and property, of licentiousness and gambling, as well as of insanity and pauperism, that are directly traceable to lives of vice. . . . To deal with this advancing demoralization, the municipal police, however honest or well-disposed, seem to a great extent inadequate. . . . It is apparent that public decency and order and public justice require the maintenance of an executive body which shall not be controlled by the public sentiment of any locality; which shall be competent in its spirit, its discipline and its numbers to a reasonable and judicious but just and impartial enforcement of the statutes of the commonwealth." Basing his objections on broader and more fundamental principles, he says: "I object to this bill that it detracts from the powers conferred for the common welfare upon the executive department of the commonwealth, taking therefrom practically the means of enforcing general laws, and vesting them in local officers, who are responsible only to their immediate constituents, and not to the whole people."[1]

[1] See *Report of the Constable of the Commonwealth*, 1869.

This attempt to abolish the state police force, therefore, failed, and as the prohibitory law was re-enacted in the following year, the question of abolishing it was not seriously considered until 1875, when there was a return to local option. In the meantime, however, the detective work of the force had become so important that chiefly for this reason it was now decided to reörganize and decrease the force, but not to abolish it. The experienced detectives of the state force had proved very valuable in working up difficult cases and in assisting local authorities in the detection of criminals. To the inexperienced authorities of the smaller towns this service was peculiarly helpful. While the state police had been established and retained for the special purpose of suppressing vice in the large cities, it was now retained very largely because of the inefficient administration of the towns.

The State Detective Force, 1875–79. The state police force was reorganized as the state detective force.[1] The governor and council were given power to appoint and remove a chief of the force and not more than thirty detectives. These officers were given the right to exercise throughout the commonwealth all the powers of police, and all the powers of constables, except the service of civil process. It was made their duty to aid the attorney-general, district-attorneys and magistrates, in the pursuit of criminals and in procuring evidence for their conviction. The governor was given power at all times to command their assistance in suppressing riots and in preserving the peace. All local police officers were required, within their respective cities and towns, to render aid, when called upon, to the governor and the state detectives.

During the first year the force numbered fifteen. It made 396 arrests and assisted the state board of charities in 273 cases. In the following year it was given charge of the

---

[1] *Acts*, 1875, 15.

enforcement of all laws relating to the hours of labor.[1] The next year an act was passed providing for various safety appliances in all factories and public buildings.[2] It was made the duty of the chief of the detective force to detail one or more of his force to act as inspectors of factories and public buildings, and to see that the law was observed.[3] The state inspectors were also required by this statute to enforce all laws regulating the employment of women and minors in manufacturing establishments. By this provision the work of local truant officers in enforcing the compulsory school law was greatly facilitated.

In 1878, the state having become infested with bands of tramps who were little better than brigands, it was made the special duty of the detective force to enforce the law against vagrancy.[4] In this year the force numbered thirty, the maximum number allowed by the law. Three of this number were specially detailed for the inspection of factories and public buildings. The rest of the force was employed in the detection and prevention of all manner of crimes. They performed special service at military musters, camp-meetings, agricultural fairs and other public gatherings. In this year 1,100 arrests were made for all degrees of crime, and stolen property to the value of $106,204.70 was recovered.[5]

The Massachusetts District Police. A strong antagonism against a state police had however been aroused, and an attempt was made in the following year to abolish it and transfer its duties relative to labor laws and the inspection of

[1] *Acts*, 1876, 216.

[2] *Ibid.*, 1877, 214.

[3] As Boston and several other cities had already provided regulations, and inspectors for their enforcement, similar to all but one of the provisions of this law, these cities were exempted from the jurisdiction of the state inspectors.

[4] *Acts*, 1878, 160.

[5] *Report of the Chief of the State Detective Force*, 1878.

factories and public buildings to the bureau of labor statistics. This attempt was unsuccessful, but the force was reorganized and greatly reduced in number.[1] It now became known as the Massachusetts district police. The governor was authorized to appoint not more than two officers in each of the eight attorneys' districts, and to designate one of the number as chief of the force. Their powers were, like those of their predecessors, to extend throughout the state, and the governor might command their services in suppressing riots and in preserving the peace. The only material change in their powers was that they were not given authority to require the assistance of the local police officers in the performance of their duties.

On account of an insufficient appropriation the new force was organized with but nine members, but the next year it was increased to sixteen, the maximum number allowed by law. Four of these were detailed as inspectors. The force has been gradually increased until now it numbers forty-four. The increase has been made necessary by the constantly increased duties that have been imposed by law upon the inspectors. In 1888 the force was divided into two departments, an inspection and a detective department.[2] The act provides that no inspector shall be required to perform duties other than those pertaining to the office of inspector of factories and public buildings, unless his services are required by the governor in suppressing riots and in preserving the peace. In 1897 there were thirty-one officers in the inspection department, and thirteen in the detective department.

Inspection Department. Among the more important duties of this department are the enforcement of the various laws relative to the employment, payment, and hours of labor of workmen and of women and children; the guarding of machinery; the sanitation and ventilation of factories and

[1] *Acts*, 1879, 305.   [2] *Ibid.*, 1888, 113.

public buildings; the supervision of tenement clothing manufacture; the heating of street cars; the inspection of steam
boilers;[1] the examination and licensing of engineers and
firemen; and the inspection of elevators, except in the city
of Boston. Except in the city of Boston, also, the inspectors
are required to enforce the provisions of the law relative to
the security of the occupants of factories and public buildings in case of fire, and the plans of proposed buildings
subject to the law are required to be submitted to the inspector of the district. The mayor and aldermen of all cities
except Boston, and the selectmen of towns, have the right to
call upon a state inspector to inspect buildings considered
dangerous to life or limb. It is the duty of the inspectors of
cities and towns to report the condition of fire-escape appliances in hotels and lodging houses to the chief of the district
police; and accidents occurring to employees must also be
reported to this officer by all manufacturing and mercantile
establishments.

In the enforcement of these various provisions the chief of
the detective force, subject to the approval of the governor,
is given certain ordinance powers, and the inspectors are
given a large degree of discretion. Any person may appeal
from the order of an inspector to a justice of the superior
court. The justice may hear and decide the case himself, or
refer it to three disinterested experts; and the order of the
inspector may be affirmed, modified, or annulled.[2]

It is thus seen that in this very broad field of regulation
the commonwealth assumes directly the execution of its laws.
It does not leave their enforcement to the option of the local-

[1] Steam boilers that are under the periodically guaranteed inspection of insurance companies are exempt from inspection by the state inspector. Here business
interest and public interest coincide; the company not only inspects, but *guaran-
tees* its inspection.

[2] See *Acts*, 1894, chapters 481 and 508; *Acts*, 1895, chapters 136, 418, and 471;
Acts, 1896, 546.

ities, nor does it attempt to force unwilling local officials to execute them; it deals directly with the individuals and corporations whose affairs are to be regulated.   In this it deals with public corporations (cities and towns) in the same way that it deals with private corporations.   It regulates the employment of laborers by cities and towns, and the sanitation and ventilation of their public buildings in substantially the same manner that it regulates employment, sanitation and ventilation in factories.   The work of the state inspectors in improving the ventilation of schools has been particularly valuable.

Detective Department.   The chief duty of this department is to aid the attorney-general, the local police authorities, and especially the district attorneys in the detection, arrest and conviction of criminals.   This work of the force is especially valuable to the towns, whose officers are inexperienced in detective work.   Of this the chief of the force speaks as follows:[1]

"The increase in crime, and especially in the number of burglaries during the past year in the towns throughout the commonwealth, is a strong argument in favor of a force large enough to cope with the criminal work.   That local town officers often fail to ferret out crime is not surprising, when it is considered that in a majority of cases the cities furnish the class that commit these depredations, and when undetected they return to their haunts. * * * * I am decidedly of the opinion, that, in cities where there is always an established police force, the services of state officers are seldom required; but, for the prevention of crime or detection of criminals in the towns of the state, officers trained for detective work are indispensable."

Every year numerous requests are made by local authorities and associations for the services of state detectives at

[1] *Report of the Chief of the Massachusetts District Police*, 1880, p. 4.

large public gatherings, such as public celebrations, military encampments, and agricultural fairs. The state detectives, knowing the professional thieves and pickpockets who are accustomed to frequent such places, are enabled to render efficient service, while the local officers are almost powerless. Besides this strictly detective work, one member of the force is detailed for duty in connection with the coast fisheries.[1]

The Suppression of Disorder. In the district police the governor is furnished with a force that can be instantly summoned by him to act in any part of the state for the suppression of disorder and the preservation of the peace. By the timely use of this force disturbances have been suppressed which might otherwise have developed into dangerous riots, destructive to life and property. With the arrival of the state force the tendency to disorder and violence has been checked. Though the state force has been weak in numbers, no turbulent crowd has yet ventured to test its strength.

In the year that the district police was organized (1879), and when it numbered but nine men, it was ordered to Fall River on account of the labor troubles there and rendered most valuable service. The employers concerned testify to its service, as follows:[2] "A change for the better, and in favor of law and order was noticeable immediately after their arrival, attributable, we believe, to the fact that the disturbing element recognized in the district police a force entirely independent of local political influence, ready to see the law executed without fear or favor." The mayor of the city, in commending the work of the force in a letter to the chief, says:[3] "No matter how good a local force of police a place may have, I am convinced that officers wearing the state authority have a moral influence in any community far

[1] *Acts*, 1897, 288.

[2] *Report of the Chief of the Massachusetts District Police*, 1879, p. 4.

[3] *Ibid.*, p. 3.

superior to the best local police whenever any general
tendency to violate the law or create a disturbance exists. I
have had some opportunity to see the working of the state
police in its various forms in this city, and I do not hesitate
to say that twice as many men, known to and knowing
almost every person in the city, could not be as effective
in preserving public order as the force under your direction."

Two years later the force prevented serious trouble from
developing during a strike of canal laborers in the town of
Sandwich.[1] During the year 1885 it was summoned to three
towns on account of anticipated disturbances arising from
strikes among factory operatives.[2] In the towns of Ran-
dolph and Rockland the state police appeared and made a
few arrests, after which the excitement subsided. At Mill-
ville disgraceful rows and assaults preceded the call for the
services of the state force, but upon its arrival the disturbance was at once suppressed. On two occasions, in 1889,
the force was called to Buzzard's Bay to enforce the laws in
relation to fisheries. In 1893 it was called to North Abington
on account of trouble between the town and a railroad company. In the present year (1898) the force has been called
to New Bedford during a strike of cotton mill operatives.

During the past twenty years there have been many long
and bitter struggles between labor and capital in Massachusetts; that they have never led to the destruction of life and
property is perhaps largely due to the existence of a state
police.[3] By its prompt action incipient riots have been suppressed, and the mere knowledge of its existence has exerted
a repressive influence that can scarcely be overestimated.
A local police, subject as it must be to personal and local

---

[1] *Ibid.*, 1881, p. 6.   [2] *Ibid.*, 1885, p. 9.

[3] During all this period the state militia has been called upon for but one day's
service on account of labor troubles. February 21, 1887, two companies were
called out during a strike at Cambridge.

influences, cannot exert the repressive influence that is more potent than actual physical force in dealing with turbulence; the *posse comitatus* of the sheriff is an unreliable and often dangerous expedient; the militia is unwieldy, expensive and inefficient.[1] In its state police Massachusetts has the most efficient means of suppressing disorder that has yet been developed in any American commonwealth.

II. *The Investigation of Fires*

The establishment of state police supervision for the investigation of fires has been made necessary to prevent the setting of fires for the purpose of defrauding the insurance companies. Were the insurance companies the final losers, they might be relied upon to take care of themselves; but the rate-making association of the companies levies a tax upon the whole community, sufficient in the long run to repair the effects of carelessness and crime. The competition between companies is now so great that they make little attempt to investigate suspicious fires for fear that such action may have the appearance of an attempt to avoid the payment of rightful claims, and thus prejudice them in the public mind. Nor have the local police proved equal to the demands of the occasion. They have usually considered it a matter between the company and the individual, totally unmindful of the public injury involved. Especially in the smaller cities and towns, personal considerations and influences usually prevent any thorough investigation.[2]

The first movement in the direction of state control was made in 1886.[3] The act authorized the governor, with the

---

[1] Had Pennsylvania possessed a state police the recent tragedy near Hazleton could scarcely have occurred.

[2] See *Official Fire Inquests :* an address by Chas. W. Whitcomb, state fire marshal of Massachusetts, before the annual convention of the fire underwriter's association of the northwest, held at Chicago, 1895.

[3] *Acts*, 1886, 354.

consent of the council, to appoint a fire marshal for the city of Boston. The city was reimbursed by the state for the salary that it was required to pay him. It was his duty to investigate the cause of every fire, to cause an inquest to be held in suspicious cases, and to prosecute incendiaries. Though appointed by the governor and council, and removable by the governor, he was placed under the supervision and direction of the city board of fire commissioners.

In 1888 it was made the duty of the board of fire engineers of every city except Boston, and the selectmen of every town to investigate the cause of every fire. But for reasons already given this attempt to secure local action was largely unsuccessful. This failure, together with the beneficial results achieved by the fire marshal of Boston, led to the creation of the office of state fire marshal in 1894.[1] The office of fire marshal of Boston was abolished and its efficient occupant was made state fire marshal. The local boards are still required to make investigations as under the former law of 1888; but the fire marshal may if he deems necessary supervise and direct their investigations, and they are now required to make a report to him within a week after the occurrence of the fire. The state is divided into ten districts, and an assistant of the state marshal is stationed in each district. Upon receiving the report of the local board, the district officer at once proceeds to an investigation of the cause of the fire, and reports to the state marshal. If any evidence of incendiarism is shown an inquest is held, and if the facts warrant an arrest is made and the offender prosecuted.[2] The state fire marshal and also the local boards have the right to inspect buildings and to order the removal of combustible materials or inflammable conditions. But in

[1] *Acts*, 1894, 444.

[2] *First Report of the State Fire Marshal*, 1894.

case the order is given by a local board the owner may appeal to the state fire marshal and he may revoke the order.

III. *Enforcement of Law in the Rural Towns*

The prevalence of lawlessness in the declining rural towns of western Massachusetts has recently received a good deal of attention.   It is charged that ruffianism is almost unchecked, and that the local constables are little more than figureheads.   Mr. W. M. Cook, who has made a careful statistical investigation of murders in Massachusetts, finds that the four counties of western Massachusetts, Franklin, Hampshire, Hampden and Berkshire, have decidedly the worst record.   In Franklin, the county that has the blackest record, there are but three towns of more than three thousand inhabitants, and seventeen out of twenty-six towns show a decrease in population during the past twenty years.   In the last ten years twenty-six of the thirty-two towns of Berkshire county have declined in population.   Mr. Cook says that " the more atrocious and flagrant murders were hidden away in the more remote localities, in general following the line of least resistance."   In explaining the bad record of these western counties he says :[1]

"The best stock of the old families has been leaving the hillside farms for years and going to the west or to the cities. The least desirable of the old native stock has been left at home.   Population has dwindled, and the consequent intermarriages between relatives have perhaps caused deterioration in many families.   Then, again, very many rural towns have been left isolated by the railroads ; the churches have grown weak and of little account as a barrier against social degeneration.   The solitude of rural life leaves men more a prey to brooding over real or fancied wrongs or grievances. Finally, the lack of police restraint in small towns allows

[1] *Publications of the American Statistical Association*, v. 3, p. 357.

ample scope to unbridled passions and to innate ferocity. Perhaps this lack of close police supervision is a very considerable factor in the bad record of the rural Massachusetts districts as regards homicide. It would be unwarranted to say that the rural population has a stronger innate tendency to commit murder than the population of the metropolis."

The *Springfield Republican* has recently published interviews with the sheriffs of these western counties, all of whom acknowledge that hoodlumism exists to an alarming extent.[1] The sheriff of one county explains that "the constables have personal interests to look after, and they are almost always anxious to escape the duties of investigating a case or of making an arrest that is unpopular." Another sheriff says, "I have taken a three days' trip in the county, and I could not help but notice the careless ways in which matters were conducted. I feel in general that there is too little care in selecting the selectmen of the towns, and in turn the selection of constables or officers. The offices often go begging, no doubt, and in this way men are put in who are not the best for the place. I sometimes think that if in these country towns there was any great emergency, which would call for courage, the officials would be found lacking sadly in backbone."

As a result of these disclosures, the plan is being agitated of placing one or more state police in each county for the enforcement of the law whenever the town constable neglects or refuses to act.

IV. *Metropolitan Police*

Although from the facts given above, it would seem that the rural towns were more in need of state interference, it is in certain cities alone that the control of the police has been taken out of the hands of the local authorities and vested in

---

[1] *Springfield Republican*, August 26, 1897.

state officials. This peculiar condition has doubtless resulted from an exaggeration of the evils of city government, and an enshrinement of New England town government based largely on departed virtues.

The police force of Boston passed under the control of a centrally appointed board in 1885,[1] and that of Fall River in 1894.[2] The provisions of both acts are substantially the same. A board of three members is appointed by the governor and council, and is subject to removal by them. The members must be appointed from the two principal political parties, and must be residents of the city. Their salaries are paid by the city, and they are not allowed to engage in any other business. The board is given power to appoint and organize the police force of the city, and to make all necessary rules and regulations for its government. All necessary expenses incurred by the board in the maintenance of buildings, the payment of the patrolmen and for incidental purposes must be paid by the city upon the requisition of the board; but the number or pay of the patrolmen cannot be increased without the authorization of the city council. In case of riot or violent disturbance, the mayor may assume control of the police; and the board of police is required to execute the orders issued by him for the suppression of the disturbance. The board also has control over the granting of liquor licenses.

The influences which brought about the passage of these acts were substantially the same as those which were behind the attempt to establish the metropolitan system previous to 1865.[3] Aside from a general distrust in the capacity of large cities for self-government, there is a special distrust of their ability to deal with the liquor problem and the suppression of vice. It may be doubted, however, admitting that

---

[1] *Acts*, 1885, 323.   [2] *Ibid.*, 1894, 351.   [3] See above, p. 81.

it is expedient for the state to interfere in these matters, whether the central control of the city police is the best means of accomplishing that end.   The substitution of a state board for a board or official under immediate control of the mayor and the city council introduces a disorganizing element into city government.   It is a return to the irresponsible and now generally discarded " board system."   The state board being largely independent in its expenditure of city money, considerable friction is sure to result between it and the city council, that is held responsible for the tax levy and the appropriation of the revenue.   This leads to numerous appeals to the legislature to interfere.

But more important still is the fact that the work of the police department is so intimately connected with the work of almost every other city department, that unless they are all under the supervision of a single head the most efficient organization cannot be secured.   The suppression of vice and the regulation of the liquor traffic form but a small part of the duty of a city police force.   If it is desirable for the state to interfere in these matters, the best plan would seem to be that adopted between 1865 and 1875 ; the enforcement of such state laws as the local police neglect to enforce through a small force of state police, while leaving the local police under the control of the local authorities.   This, moreover, is the plan which is now proposed for the enforcement of law in the rural districts.

To be sure, the local police are very largely employed in the enforcement of state laws, yet from this it by no means follows that they should be state officials.   The question of state or local enforcement of a state regulation turns largely upon the cause which brought about its enactment.   If the state intervenes in order to compel action which is opposed to the public sentiment existing in certain municipalities, it is unwise to turn over the enforcement of the regulations to the authorities of the municipality. But laws of this kind are very exceptional; the great bulk of police legislation is enacted by the state, rather than by the municipality, almost wholly in the interest of uniformity. There is no class of criminally disposed municipalities as there is of individuals; were the municipalities left to themselves they could be trusted to enact the necessary legislation to preserve peace, order and security. Their laws, however, would not be uniform, and this, in a mobile society, would cause great inconvenience; to secure uniformity the state intervenes. In the enforcement of these laws, however, there is a complete identity of interest between the municipality and the state. There is no inconsistency, therefore, in turning them over to the municipalities for enforcement.

CHAPTER VII

TAXATION

THE purpose of this chapter is to review briefly the history of the apportionment of the state general property tax among the towns, to trace the progress in the disintegration of the general property tax and to note the tendency toward a separation of state from local taxation.

1. *Apportionment of the General Property Tax*

The general property tax has from the start been the back-bone of the revenue systems of both the central and the local governments. It was soon supplemented by a poll tax and a "faculties" or income tax, and also by customs duties, excises and lotteries.[1] At first the general court determined the amount that each town should raise, and this amount, together with the amounts necessary for local purposes, was re-apportioned by the town officers among the individuals of the town. It is not known upon what the first apportionments made by the general court were based; they were probably based on the valuations of the local officers, corrected in accordance with the best judgment of the members of the court. In 1636, however, a committee of thirteen was named by the general court with authority to require the assessment lists of each town, and with these and all other means at their command to determine upon a true valuation for each town. Upon the valuations thus determined the general court based its apportionments for a num-

---

[1] Douglas, *Financial History of Massachusetts*, pp. 16–35.

ber of years, probably until about 1645. About this time the plan of apportionment by the general court appears to have ceased, and the colony rates were levied by the local officials upon valuations made by them. Some degree of centralization was, however, provided. In 1646 a system of county equalization was established. Each town chose one man who, together with the selectmen, made the assessment. The representatives of the towns thus chosen met in the shire town, and after examining into "the truth and equity" of the assessment of each town, revised and equalized the assessments according to their best judgment.[1]

No provision was yet made for equalization between the counties, and complaints of inequality were rife. The difficulties in the way of equitably assessing the property tax over the entire commonwealth were thus early demonstrated. Already, towns were vying with towns, and counties with counties, in the undervaluation of their property; and each was satisfied that the other was escaping its just proportion of the common burdens. To avoid this evil, in 1668 there was established one of the most thorough-going schemes of general equalization that have ever been provided.[2] A board of equalization was established and given the final and absolute determination of the valuation of the property of each town and of each individual. The law reads as follows:

"Whereas sundry complaints have been made of much inequality in the annual assessments to public charges, the several towns and counties not paying in just proportion to one another, as is the true intent of the law, . . . it is therefore ordered, . . . that henceforth from time to time there shall be some meet, able, faithful and judicious men, chosen and authorized by the court, viz., two in the county of Essex, two in Suffolk, two in Middlesex, and two in Norfolk, who

[1] Douglas, *Financial History of Massachusetts*, pp. 23–26.
[2] *Colony Records*, v. iv, pt. 2, p. 363.

meeting together with the commissioners of the several towns, they, or the major part of them so met together, shall have the absolute and final determination of the just proportion of each town and of each person and estate therein, so that there may be a just and equal proportion between county and county, town and town, merchants and husbandmen, with all other handicrafts as much as in them lie."

This law continued until the annulment of the colony charter, and probably until the granting of the new charter in 1692. The last application of the principle appears under the temporary law of 1692.[1] As soon as general equalization ceased, the inequalities that at once resulted brought about a return to the system of the apportionment between the towns by the general court of the amount to be raised. The first apportionment act of 1694 recites that the assessors of the towns do not properly perform their duties, and that this " has occasioned an inequality and disproportion betwixt town and town." To obviate this the act definitely fixes the amount to be raised by each town for the support of the general government.[2] The plan then adopted was continued down to 1871. At periods of from one to ten years new apportionments have been made by the general court; the usual period has been between five and ten years. Up to 1707 these apportionments appear to have been based upon the assessments of the local assessors as equalized for each county by the town representatives, as under the law of 1646. For the next two apportionments, made in 1718 and 1727, a more centralized plan was adopted. The general court appointed three commissioners for each county to examine and revise the assessment lists of the towns.[3] After 1727 the general court continued to make new apportion-

---

[1] *Province Laws*, v. 1, p. 91.

[2] *Ibid.*, v. 1, p. 177.   [3] *Ibid.*, v. 2, pp. 106, 419.

ments at irregular intervals, based upon the returns made by
the town assessors.

The constitution of the commonwealth, adopted in 1780,
provides that for the proper apportionment of the state tax,
"there shall be a valuation of estates, within the commonwealth, taken anew once in every ten years at least, and as
much oftener as the general court shall order."[1] Under
this provision the practice continued much the same as before 1780. At intervals of about ten years, until 1871, the
general court has ordered the town assessors to make returns to it of all property liable to taxation. The custom
has been for a large committee of the general court, with the
aid of these returns, the valuations fixed by local assessors
in preceding years, and their own knowledge of local conditions, to determine the valuation of each town, and from
that to fix the proportion of the state tax that each town shall
pay, until a new apportionment be made. The towns have
then levied the amount thus definitely determined, upon valuations made by their own assessors.[2]

The decennial apportionment was a prodigious task for
the legislative committees. The report of the committee for
1793 gives a good idea of the nature of the undertaking and
the methods employed:[3]

"In forming this estimate your committee were regulated
by the income of the property, as deducible from the different kinds and quantity of produce apparent from said
returns—making allowance for circumstances of locality and
other appendages, as to them appeared reasonable, and having completed this, your committee found that from the
errors and deficiencies in the returns from many towns, the
relative proportions of such towns to those which had made

---

[1] *Constitution*, ch. i., art. 4, sec. 1.

[2] County taxes were apportioned on the same basis as state taxes.

[3] Resolves of 1792–3, c. 196.

legal and proper returns, would be marked with striking features of injustice—to remedy which your committee proceeded to add such articles and amount of property not included in the returns, as by their best judgment deliberately used, it appeared the inhabitants of the different places must be possessed of."

Down to 1860 the apportionments had ordinarily been made every ten years. About this time, however, a very pronounced readjustment of wealth and population began. Some towns rapidly increased in population and wealth while others steadily declined; population was being concentrated in cities, while the rural hill towns were being depopulated. Under such conditions apportionment but once in ten years could not fail to work great injustice. From 1860 to 1883, therefore, apportionments were made about every five years, and since 1883 they have been made every three years.

Not till 1871 did the system of apportionment by legislative committees give way to the present system of apportionment by the state tax commissioner.[1] Apportionment had constantly been becoming a more and more difficult task. Under the simple, uniform conditions of an eighteenth century agricultural community, it was a comparatively simple matter. Now the great disparity in economic conditions and the great multiplicity and intricacy of industrial and commercial relations, made it an all but impossible task. For this work the large legislative committees were most cumbersome, expensive and inefficient. Their apportionments were certain to be the joint product of guess-work and log-rolling.

Since 1871, therefore, the tax commissioner has taken the place of the legislative committee. Once every three years

[1] *Acts*, 1871, 125.

the local assessors return to the tax commissioner full copies of their assessment books.[1] This officer takes these books and analyzes them so as to show the average assessed valuation of the different classes of property in each city and town.   In addition to this he has an abstract taken of the registries of all mortgages and of all real estate conveyed that seem to give the consideration for the conveyance.[2] By comparing the average assessed valuations of the different classes of property in the different towns, and by comparing assessed valuations with the value as shown in actual transfers, the tax commissioner determines by what per cent. to increase or reduce the assessed valuation of each of the 353 cities and towns.   Upon this basis he then apportions to each the amount that it shall be required to pay of every one thousand dollars of state and county taxes.   He reports this apportionment to the legislature, and it has been the custom for that body to adopt it without alteration.

In this system no attempt is made to equalize the assessments throughout the state on which the tax thus apportioned is actually levied.   It being an apportioned tax and not a percentage tax, as in most other states, this is unnecessary.   A definite amount is required of each town; the town may raise this amount by the assessment of property at full value or at but half its full value, the result will be the same.

The plan has worked fairly well in Massachusetts.   Competitive undervaluation, which is the bane of every state in which it is attempted to use real estate for purposes of both state and local taxation, is not very pronounced.   This is due partly to the system of apportionment, partly to the smaller area of the state, and partly to the fact that inde-

[1] *Acts*, 1881, 163.

[2] The abstracts of the registries made, are for the first five months of the year for which the returns of the local assessors are required.

pendent sources of state revenue have been developed and the state general property tax has come to bear very lightly on the different communities. In 1896 the state poll and property tax was but one twenty-fifth of the total poll and property taxes collected in the state; and formed less than one-third of the total taxes collected by the state government.

2. *Disintegration of the General Property Tax*

The single general property tax has been broken up into a number of separate taxes. It is slowly undergoing a process of disintegration. The plan of taxing everything according to a simple, uniform rule, broke down when applied to complex nineteenth century conditions. The first important step in the disintegration came in 1812, when a state tax was levied on the paid up capital stock of banking corporations.[1] A law of 1832 provides that the machinery and real estate of manufacturing corporations shall be assessed locally, and that in assessing the shareholders, a proportional amount of the value of the real estate and machinery thus assessed shall be deducted from the value of each share.[2] In 1862 a state tax of one-half of one per cent. was levied on the deposits of savings banks, and the depositors were exempted from both state and local taxation on their deposits. By the same act a state tax was also imposed upon the premiums or assessments of fire and marine insurance companies.

The next year it was attempted to levy a state tax on the dividends of non-resident shareholders in Massachusetts corporations by collecting it from the corporations.[3] This act was contested in the courts, and finally declared unconstitutional,[4] but in the meantime it had been repealed, and the first general law for the taxation of Massachusetts corpora-

---

[1] *Acts*, 1812, 32.   [2] *Ibid.*, 1832, 158.

[3] *Ibid.*, 1863, 236.   [4] Oliver *v.* Mills, 11 Allen, 268.

tions had been enacted.[1] It provides for the taxation of the
real estate and machinery of all Massachusetts corporations
by the local assessors, for state and local purposes. The state
tax commissioner then determines the total market value of
the shares of the corporation, and after deducting therefrom
the amount locally assessed for real estate and machinery,
assesses the remainder at the average rate at which property
is taxed throughout the state.[2] The state retains a portion
of the tax collected equal to the proportion of the shares
held by non-residents, and distributes the remainder to the
towns in proportion to the number of shares held in each.
The object was to obtain a revenue for the state from the
shares held by non-residents, but not to deprive the towns
of the revenue that they had been deriving from the taxation
of resident shareholders.[3]

In taxing the shares of national banks, it was necessary to
provide a different system in order to comply with congres-
sional regulations. In 1868, in order to secure a revenue to

[1] *Acts*, 1864, 208.

[2] In the case of railroad, telegraph and telephone companies allowance is made
for that portion of their business carried on outside of the commonwealth.

[3] In order to prevent the town assessors from placing too high a valuation on
the real estate and machinery, thus securing to the town an unfair portion of the
tax, the tax commissioner has supervisory authority. With the exception of machinery, the tangible personal property of corporations is not locally assessed. In
the case of railroads, only real estate outside of the right of way is locally assessed.
The courts have held it unconstitutional to tax railroads on property within the
right of way and devoted to a public purpose, but a tax on the franchise is not a
tax on property (Portland Bank *v.* Apthorp, 12 Mass., 252). The question of the
taxation of railroad property first came up in the case of Worcester *v.* The Western Railroad, 4 Met., 564. The court says: " it is manifest that the establishment of that great thoroughfare is regarded as a public work, established by
public authority, intended for the public use and benefit, the use of which is
secured to the whole community, and constitutes therefore, like a canal, turnpike
or highway, a public easement. The only principle on which the legislature
could have authorized the taking of private property for its construction, without
the owner's consent, is, that it was for the public use."

the state from the shares of non-residents, it was provided that
a tax upon their shares should be collected from the banks
by the local authorities.[1]   Shares held by residents continued
to be assessed upon the individual holders, as in the case of
other personal property.   The superiority of the method of
collecting the tax through the corporation itself, already
demonstrated in the workings of the corporation tax act of
1864, soon led to its application to national banks.   The law
of 1871 provides for the levying of a tax by the local assessors upon the total market value of the shares less the value
of the real estate.[2]   The method of distributing the amount
collected between the state and the cities and towns is the
same as in the case of other corporations.

Another important modification of the general property
tax came in 1881.   According to the method of the general
property tax, the attempt was made to tax both the real
estate and the mortgage upon it.   The law of 1881 is de-
signed to bring about the taxation of real estate once, and
only once, whether it be mortgaged or not.   It leaves the
question as to who shall pay the tax upon the mortgage to
be settled between the mortgageor and mortgagee, the result
being that the owner of the property usually contracts to
pay the tax.

In 1891 a state collateral inheritance tax was levied.   In-
ventories of all estates liable to the tax are filed with the
register of probate and mailed by that officer to the treasurer
of the commonwealth.   By means of this inventory or of an
appraisement made by appraisers appointed by the judge of
probate, the treasurer of the commonwealth assesses
the tax.

It is thus evident that the general property tax has under-
gone a considerable disintegration, and its present unsatis-

Acts, 1868, 242.   [2] *Ibid.*, 1871, 390.

factory condition appears to make further disintegration inevitable. The general property tax in Massachusetts has always been in theory a general income tax; and it has actually been a combined property and income tax. In case a person derived his income from property, tangible or intangible, the value of the property was considered the best gauge of his income, but in case his income was derived from a trade or profession, he was taxed on his income just as if it had been so much real estate or personal property. It is in the taxation of intangible property and income that the general property tax has broken down most completely.

The income tax applies to the excess of income over two thousand dollars derived from any trade, profession or employment. Although the statute declares that incomes derived from property subject to taxation shall not be taxed, the court has held that this does not exempt the income of merchants derived from their business.[1] The tax is quite unpopular and from a revenue standpoint is of little importance. In 1895, 242 towns taxed no income whatever. It has been impossible to obtain the figures for Boston and Somerville, but the total income assessed in the other cities and towns amounted to but $5,409,925, This amount taxed at the average rate would bring in an aggregate revenue of about eighty thousand dollars.[2] The tax commission reports that this partial income tax "has proved no less difficult of satisfactory administration than the other parts of the present method of taxing intangible personalty."[3] Concerning the attempted taxation of intangible personalty the same commission says: "The taxation of this form of property is in high degree uncertain, irregular, and unsatisfactory. It rests mainly on guess work; it is blind, and therefore unequal.

---

[1] Wilcox *v*. Middlesex Commissioners, 103 Mass., 544.

[2] See *Report of the Tax Commission*, 1897, pp. 47–51.

[3] *Ibid.*, p. 109.

Here is its greatest evil, though not its only evil. It is haphazard in its practical working, and hence demoralizing alike to tax payers and tax officials."[1] The commission therefore recommends the abolition of the partial income tax and of the tax on intangible personalty, and the substitution of a general inheritance tax and of a habitation tax.

With the disintegration of the general property tax, the tendency has been more and more toward a separation of state from local taxation; the state has obtained a constantly increasing portion of its revenue from corporation and inheritance taxes, while the taxation of real estate has been left more and more exclusively to the municipalities. At present the cities and towns levy and collect the general property tax, the poll tax and the tax on national banks, and pay part of the proceeds to the state; the state levies and collects the corporation tax and distributes part of the proceeds to the cities and towns, while it taxes savings banks, insurance companies, and collateral inheritances, and retains the entire proceeds. With the more complete disintegration of the general property tax which is impending, it seems very probable that certain of the resulting taxes will be reserved to the municipalities, while others will be used exclusively by the central government.

Some segregation of the sources of revenue seems to follow naturally from their varying natures. Among a number of different taxes it is to be expected that some will prove peculiarly appropriate for local and others for state purposes. This is unquestionably a fact. There are certain taxes that are peculiarly adapted to municipal administration and there are others that are peculiarly adapted to commonwealth administration. A real estate tax cannot be uniformly administered over an extensive area; it is best adapted to

[1] *Report of the Tax Commission*, 1897, p. 59.

local administration. On the other hand, it is evident that taxes upon inheritance and upon inter-municipal corporations can not be successfully administered by a government whose jurisdiction extends over but a small area. Such a separation is reinforced by the fact that each of these two governments in the exercise of its peculiar functions stands in a special relation to certain economic interests. Certain economic interests are more vitally and immediately affected by the activities of the municipality, and certain others by the activities of the commonwealth. The value of real estate is to a considerable extent created and maintained by the activities of the municipality; while on the other hand corporations receive their charters from the state, and the right of inheritance is secured by the state.

CHAPTER VIII

STREET RAILWAYS

THE development of street railways in Massachusetts began in 1853 with the incorporation of two companies by special acts of the legislature.[1] One of these began operations between Boston and Cambridge in the spring of 1856 and the other between Boston and Roxbury a few months later. The relation of the street railway to the municipality, set forth in these special acts, was followed, in most respects, by subsequent special and general acts for many years and in certain important respects has continued down to the present time.

It was provided that the acts should be void unless accepted by the city councils of the cities affected. After a public hearing the mayor and aldermen might grant locations or franchises for the laying of tracks ; and, at any time after the expiration of one year from the completion of the road, the mayor and aldermen might revoke any franchise thus granted.[2] Street railways were felt to be a very doubtful experiment, and this provision was intended as a safeguard to compel the removal of the tracks from the street in case they became a public nuisance. Although the street railway soon came to be recognized as necessary and permanent, the certain measure of utility in this provision has secured its continuance down to the present time. The cities were authorized after the expiration of ten years to purchase the roads by paying a sum sufficient to reimburse the stockholders

[1] *Acts*, 1853, 353, 383. [2] *Ibid.*, 1854, 94.

for the par value of their shares and to secure to them, together with their dividends, an annual return of ten per cent. for the period during which they had held the shares. The aldermen had power to make regulations concerning the speed of cars, the use of tracks and similar matters. The companies were required to make annual returns to the secretary of the commonwealth in the manner required of steam railroads.

In 1864 the first general law regulating street railways was passed. In most respects it simply follows the principles previously adopted in the special acts. No provision is made for municipal purchase of the roads, however, and it is provided that no company shall sell or lease its road except with the permission of the legislature. Furthermore, the first attempt at regulation by a state commission is here made. Upon complaint of the aldermen or selectmen, or of fifty voters of a city or town, the supreme judicial court is authorized to appoint three commissioners, who, after a public hearing, may revise and regulate street railway fares, but in so doing the profits of the road cannot be reduced to less than ten per cent. of its actual cost of construction. A similar commission may also be provided in case one company desires to use the tracks of another, and they are unable to agree upon terms.[1]

By this time the street railway had come to be recognized as necessary and permanent, and it was urged that investments should be made more secure than they could be while the franchise was revocable at the pleasure of the aldermen or selectmen. Accordingly a special commission was appointed to consider the relation of the street railways to the cities and towns. The commission reported that they did not deem the laws of the business sufficiently settled to

---

[1] *Acts*, 1864, 229.

define strictly the proper relation of the municipality to the
street railway. They considered, however, that although
the municipality should have considerable freedom of action,
it would be best to provide a permanent railroad commission,
to which appeals might be carried in certain cases, and
which should exercise broad powers over both steam and
street railroads.[1]

A railroad commission was established in 1869, and
though its powers were few and weak, their judicious exercise has proved most beneficial.[2]   It consists of three salaried
members, appointed and removable by the governor and
council.   Their term of office is three years; and the method
of partial renewal is adopted, the term of one member
expiring annually.

By the law of 1869 and the amendments to it during the
two following years, the commission was given a general supervision over all railroads and street-railways. Its most
important power was that in the interest of publicity. Railway companies were required to furnish the commission
all information requested, and to make annual returns to
the commission according to the forms prescribed by it.[3]
The companies were required to report all railway accidents,
and it was made the duty of the commission to investigate their
cause. Whenever in the opinion of the commission improved facilities or reduced fares were demanded on any railway, it was made its duty to call the fact to the attention of the
company; and upon the petition of the aldermen or selectmen, or of twenty voters, it was made the duty of the commission to investigate any complaint against a company, and if
the complaint was well founded to recommend to the company
the correction of the abuse, and also to report the facts to
the legislature. The power, with important limitations, to

---

[1] *House Documents*, 1865, no. 15.

[2] *Acts*, 1869, 408.   [3] *Ibid.*, 1870, 382.

order a reduction of fares and to determine the terms upon which one company might use the tracks of another, which had hitherto rested with special commissions appointed by the supreme judicial court, was now transferred to the railroad commission.[1] It was made the duty of the commission to notify the attorney-general in case it believed any company to be violating the law.[2]

Up to 1874 every street railway had been incorporated by a special act of the legislature. Previous to this the struggles of contending companies for privileges in the streets of Boston and other cities had necessarily taken place before the committees of the legislature. The legislature determined who should and who should not be permitted to receive locations for their tracks from the board of aldermen. The aldermen could then grant a location or refuse it as they saw fit. The general incorporation law of this year provides that a certain number of individuals, *after* receiving the grant of a location by the aldermen or selectmen of a municipality, and fulfilling the usual conditions, shall receive a certificate of incorporation from the secretary of the commonwealth.[3] This act also authorizes the commission to permit a railway corporation to increase its capital stock beyond the amount prescribed in its charter. This general law did not prevent street railway companies from incorporating under special acts if for any reason they chose to do so, and could prevail upon the legislature to comply with their desires. At present almost as many companies are incorporated by special acts as under the general law.

Two years later the commission was authorized to examine the books and accounts of railways from time to time in order to see that they were being kept in the manner that it had prescribed.[4] It was also authorized to require railways

[1] *Acts*, 1871, 381.   [2] *Ibid.*, 1870, 382.

[3] *Ibid.*, 1874, 29.   [4] *Ibid.*, 1876, 185.

to publish statements of their financial condition at such times as it deemed proper; and on application of a director or of persons owning one-fiftieth part of the stock, the commission was required to examine the books and financial condition of the railway and to publish the results of its investigation.

No very important changes were made in the position of the street railway from 1876 down to within the past ten years. The total street railway mileage increased from 88.8 miles in 1860, to 222.5 miles in 1880, and to 470.2 miles in 1887. Then came the enormous development in street railway building, due to the substitution of electric for horse power, which is still in progress. Electricity was first used as a motive power on the Lynn and Boston road in 1888, and in 1889 the Boston and Revere electric railway was the first to be operated wholly by electric power. Since 1887 the street railway mileage has been more than trebled, and there are now but 11.9 miles operated exclusively by horse power.[1]

The impetus given to railway building by the introduction of electric power, and the changed conditions that have resulted, have led to the enactment of a great deal of important legislation and to a considerable increase in the powers and duties of the state commission. The subject that has received more attention than any other is that of capitalization. Here the constant effort has been to prevent stock watering, or the capitalization of the franchise or earning capacity of the road. In order to accomplish this the commission has been given almost complete control over all issues of stocks and bonds. No company can increase its capital stock beyond the amount authorized in its charter without the approval of the commission. The commission deter-

[1] *Report of the Board of Railroad Commissioners*, 1897, p. 88.

mines whether the proposed increase is consistent with the public interest. If it finds the capitalization to be already greater than the value of the property, it may annex such conditions and requirements to its approval as it may deem proper.[1] The commission is also authorized to determine the amount of each separate issue of stock and bonds.[2] When new shares are issued they must first be offered to the stockholders at their market value, as estimated by the commission.[3] The commission may approve the issue of mortgage bonds and decide upon their amount and the rate of interest to be paid, but "no issue shall be authorized unless, in the opinion of such board, the value of the constructed tracks, the equipments, and the other real and personal property of the company, taken at a fair value for railroad purposes, and excluding the value of the franchise, equals or exceeds the amount of capital stock and the debt."[4]

Previous to 1897, no lease, sale or consolidation could be made except by special permission of the legislature. The commission in its report of that year recommended that something be done to facilitate the merging of the many small companies that had sprung up, holding that this " might often result in securing greater economy and efficiency of management, and in thereby giving to the public a more convenient and, in some cases, a cheaper service."[5] In accordance with this suggestion, acts were passed permitting connecting street railways to consolidate and to enter into leases and operating contracts with one another. The terms of all such consolidations and contracts must first be approved by the commission, and in the consolidation of two companies, their aggregate capitalization can in no case be

---

[1] *Acts*, 1887, 543; *Acts*, 1896, 409.   [2] *Ibid.*, 1894, 462.

[3] *Ibid.*, 1894, 472.   [4] *Ibid.*, 1889, 316.

[5] *Twenty-eighth Report of the Railroad Commissioners*, p. 106.

increased.[1] By far the most important and substantial reductions in the price of street railway transportation that
have come since its introduction in 1856, have been brought
about by increasing the distance that may be traveled for a
minimum fare, rather than in reducing the minimum. Five
cents has always been the prevailing price, but its purchasing power has been greatly increased. This has usually
come either through consolidations or extensions.

The commission can require any company to provide additional accommodations whenever it considers just and
proper.[2] It may also regulate the heating of the cars,[3] and
such fenders must be provided as it may require.[4] The
consent either of the state commission or of a special commission to be appointed by the superior court of the county,
must be obtained for the crossing at grade of railroads by
street railways, or of street railways by railroads.[5] Until
1888, the joint use of tracks by different companies was
regulated by the aldermen or selectmen. The law of this
year gives the commission a veto over the order of a local
board authorizing one company to use the tracks of another.[6] When the lines were operated by horse power, the
joint use of tracks was a comparatively simple matter, but
with the use of electric power this has become increasingly
difficult. The joint use of street railway tracks by different
companies has become almost as impractical as in the case
of steam railroads.

In 1894 three inspectors of steam railroads were appointed,
and in 1897 their duties were extended to street railways.[7]
It is their duty to investigate accidents and to see whether
the railways are complying with the laws relating to the
safety of their equipment.

The change from horse to electric power has materially

[1] *Acts*, 1897, 213, 269.   [2] *Ibid.*, 1891, 216.   [3] *Ibid.*, 1895, 136.
[4] *Ibid.*, 1895, 378.   [5] *Ibid.*, 1895, 426.   [6] *Ibid.*, 1888, 278.   [7] *Ibid.*, 1897, 376.

altered the relation of the street railway to the municipality. The old horse lines were usually included within the limits of a single city or town. Now the electric lines in eastern Massachusetts already form a continuous network between most of the cities and towns. Electric power has changed the street railway from a municipal to an inter-municipal institution. The lines operated by the Lowell, Lawrence and Haverhill Company extend through ten cities and towns, those of the West End through twelve, and those of the Lynn and Boston through eighteen. Extensions and consolidations are continually being made.[1]

The electric roads have proved dangerous competitors to the railroads, and in some respects have already practically supplanted them. During the past four years there has been an average decrease of 4,766,000 per year in the number of passengers carried by the railroads; the greater part of which has been due to a falling off in short distance traffic. The railroad commission estimates that during the past four years the suburban travel to and from Boston on the steam roads has decreased ten per cent., while that on the electric roads has increased twenty-five per cent.[2] The development of electric lines has brought railroad construction to a standstill. The commission in its report for 1896 says:[3] " From 1832, when the building of railroads in Massachusetts began, up to 1880, there were constructed in this state on an average about forty miles of railroad a year—the largest annual increment, 131 miles, occurring in 1873. In the

---

[1] Of the seventy-three companies operating lines in 1896, nineteen operated in but one municipality, seventeen in two, fifteen in three, twelve in four, three in five, two in six, two in seven, one in ten, one in twelve, and one in eighteen. *Report of the Board of Railroad Commissioners*, 1896.

[2] *Ibid.*, 1897, pp. 10–13. As competing systems of transportation have almost invariably led to combination and consolidation, this may be expected in the case of competing steam and electric lines.

[3] *Ibid.*, 1896, p. 9.

decade from 1880 to 1890, the rate was a little less than twenty miles a year. In the three years following 1890, the average fell to some eight miles; and in the last three years, less than two miles in all have been built. It appears, therefore, that for the present, so far as new lines are concerned, railroad construction in this state has practically come to an end. Additional trunk roads are no longer seriously thought of. The building of supplementary branch and cross lines seems to have been given over to the street railway companies. If the electric street railway had been discovered thirty or forty years earlier, doubtless some of the auxiliary railroad lines now in existence would never have been projected."[1]

The street railway mileage is now 1,206 miles, or 57.4 per cent. of the railroad mileage,[2] and is increasing at a more rapid rate than the railroad mileage has ever done. This development seems destined to continue until each center of population is connected with its neighbors, and a complete network of lines is thus formed throughout nearly the entire state.

With the recognition of the fact that the electric road had become an inter-municipal road, came a demand for a revision of its relations with the municipality. The power of one municipality to stand in the way of an inter-municipal road that the public convenience demanded, was considered anomalous. Moreover there was a popular feeling that the street railway companies should pay a special tax for the special privileges they enjoyed. To investigate the whole subject a special committee was appointed by the governor in July, 1897; the committee reported in February, 1898.

---

[1] In 1897 there was a decrease of 11.4 miles in the total length of railroad lines. *Ibid.*, 1897, p. 4.

[2] Length of line and not length of main track is here taken to compute railway mileage.

The committee however does not fully sympathize with the view that the street railway has become an inter-municipal institution. It holds the matter to be one " of distinctly municipal or local concernment, the community as a whole having only a broad interest in the principles involved . . . That the street railway, like the thoroughfare it partially occupies, has in many instances outgrown municipal limits, and so become an instrument of inter-urban travel and communication, is apparent, and this fact also has to be recognized as introducing new elements into the problem; but the fundamental principle of local control is thereby no more destroyed in the case of the railway than in the case of the street itself." [1]

The analogy between the highway and the railway is plausible, but deceptive. The establishment and control of highways can usually be left to the separate local divisions; unity of control is not always essential; yet even here it has been found expedient to turn over the establishment and control of distinctly inter-municipal highways to the county commissioners, and the commonwealth has recently undertaken the establishment of an extensive system of state highways. But the electric road bears a closer resemblance to the railroad than to the highway. Control can best be exercised by an authority whose jurisdiction is as extensive as the institution to be controlled. Unless this is the case the general good may be sacrificed to the selfish interests of particular localities.

At present a municipality may refuse to grant a location to a railway that would be of great public benefit. A line between neighboring cities may be blocked by the action of an intervening town. If the local authorities refuse to grant a location to a steam railroad, an appeal can be taken to the

---

[1] *Report of the Special Committee on the Relations between Cities and Towns and Street Railway Companies*, 1898, pp. 14, 15.

state commission.[1]   It seems that a similar rule should apply in the case of inter-municipal electric roads.   The same objections exist to the present power of municipalities to revoke the location of a railway.   This, too, should be exercised under the supervision of the state commission.   Though the special committee recognizes the justice of this latter position, it denies that of the former.[2]

Opinion differs as to the present legal power of municipalities to make the granting of a location or franchise conditional on the fulfilment of prescribed terms and stipulations. It may impose "restrictions," but whether this would be legally interpreted to mean "terms and conditions" is doubtful.[3]   Nevertheless, various conditions are often imposed by the municipalities as the price for obtaining a desired grant, extension, or alteration of a location.   The railroad commission reports that it does not know that a municipality has ever received direct compensation for such a purpose, and holds that it would be improper for it to do so; and it is the opinion of the commission that legally enforceable conditions cannot be imposed relative to widening or paving the street,[4] or to the amount of fare to be charged.[5]

The special committee takes a different view, holding that

---

[1] *Acts,* 1872, 53.

[2] By a special act in 1887, the railroad commission was given appellate jurisdiction over the granting and revocation of locations in Boston, Brookline, and Cambridge.   This was just previous to the introduction of electric power, and the commission was opposed to having its authority extended over what it considered was a purely municipal matter.   Now, however, under the enlarged sphere of activity of the electric road, the commission considers it eminently fitting that the authority which it has in Boston, Brookline, and Cambridge should be made general.

[3] See Cambridge *v.* Cambridge Railroad Co., 10 Allen, 50.

[4] But by general law the companies are required to pave and keep in repair the portion of the roadway between their tracks.

[5] *Report of the Board of Railroad Commissioners,* 1888, pp. 19, 174.

"under the system in use in Massachusetts it was, and it now is, in the power, as it was and is the duty, of those representing both municipalities and companies to insist on more specific and better considered grants, covering, if thought best, a given term of years, and binding in law during that term."[1] While the committee recommends that companies which have been granted a location in a municipality should be protected "from new and perhaps unreasonable conditions sought to be imposed in grants of alterations and extensions, which may be called for not less for public convenience than by corporate interest," yet it holds that municipalities should be given explicit power to impose terms and conditions on original grants of locations.[2] It is just as true that the public convenience may be thwarted in the latter case as in the former; a single town may prevent the proper development of an extensive system of transportation, or if its demands for compensation are acceded to, may impose a permanent burden upon the entire system, and indirectly on all the people that use it.

Ever since the introduction of street railways, franchises, instead of being perpetual or for a definite term of years, have been legally revocable at the pleasure of the municipality. Practically, this has led to no serious results. Promoters and investors have not been discouraged, and the railways have been able to float their bonds at a rate probably as low as if the franchises were in terms perpetual.[3] As the special committee has said, the Massachusetts franchise may be termed "a tenure during good behavior." As long as the road continues to perform a public service its franchise is

---

[1] *Report of the Special Committee on Street Railways*, 1898, pp. 22, 23.

[2] *Ibid.*, p. 23.

[3] The average rate of interest on Massachusetts railroad bonds in 1896 was 4.77 per cent.; on street railway bonds 4.98 per cent. *Report of the Board of Railroad Commissioners*, 1896, p. 10.

secure; revocation would work such great public injury that it could not be seriously considered. The railway interests prefer this system to the uncertainties of a term franchise,[1] and its continuance is of great public importance as recognizing the complete responsibility of the railway to the public in the performance of its public function.

While the sale of street railway franchises has been a source of considerable revenue to cities in other states, and especially in European countries, this has never been the case in Massachusetts. The companies are not subjected to special burdens, but are taxed in the manner that other corporations are taxed. The theory has been that the street railways should neither be subjected to peculiar burdens nor permitted to earn exceptionally large profits. If exorbitant profits exist, the remedy has been held to lie in improved facilities or cheaper service. Transportation is one of the most vital forces in social organization; there is no public service that is more organically connected with the whole of social activity. There seems to be a growing feeling therefore that the railway, no less than the highway and the post-office, should be free from exploitation in the interest either of corporations or of governments. The railroad commission in arguing against a proposed special tax on street railways says: "A tax on the carrier is a tax on the passenger. . . . Nothing has hitherto been more free than the use of the highways, for all persons, and for all purposes of travel or transportation. There is no good reason why the person who travels in a street car should pay directly or indirectly for the privilege of traveling on the highway, any more than the person who travels in a public coach or in his private carriage."[2]

[1] *Report of the Special Committee on Street Railways*, p. 18.

[2] *Report of the Board of Railroad Commissioners*, 1895, p. 112. An illustration of the way in which a special tax on the company may become a tax upon the

Although the railroad commission, as has already been noted, has full control over street railway accommodations, its control over fares is very limited. It may order reductions provided the profits of the company will not thereby be reduced below ten per cent. on the actual cost of construction.[1] In 1897 but one company paid as much as a ten per cent. dividend; thirty paid from 6 to 10 per cent.; nineteen paid from 2 to 5 per cent., and forty-three companies paid no dividends. The total dividends paid amounted to 6.02 per cent. of the total capital stock. The capital stock was $32,-670,273, and the funded debt $28,007,600.[2] This capitalization is probably considerably in excess of the actual cost of construction, but wise legislation and supervision have prevented the excesses that are prevalent in other states. "Using round numbers only, the capitalization per mile in stock and bonds ($46,600) is less in Massachusetts than the average ($49,500) in the New England states, not a third of what it is in New York ($177,800) or half what it is in Pennsylvania ($128,200), less than half what it is ($94,100) in the United States as a whole; and it is less than it is in Great Britain ($47,000), where both construction and appliances are far less costly and elaborate, and over-capitalization has been guarded against with the utmost care."[3]

passenger is furnished in the case of the petition of the town of Danvers for a reduction of fares on the Lynn and Boston Railway. The commission says, " We should perhaps be indisposed to recommend more than this at the present time, even if the case were stronger. The question of the financial relations of street railway companies to the cities and towns in which they are located, is under consideration, and may result in legislative action. If new requirements should be laid on the companies, this might have a necessary bearing on the question of fares. An addition of burdens and a reduction of fares at the same time, would be like ' burning a candle at both ends.' " *Ibid.,* 1897, p. 159.

[1] Providing the road is not over-capitalized this means ten per cent. on the amount of its bonds as well as of its stock.

[2] *Ibid.,* 1897, pp. 93-97.

[3] *Report of the Special Committee on Street Railways,* 1898, p. 37.   It should

The control over fares that the commission has been able to exercise under this provision has therefore never been very strong. The commission has from time to time received applications for the reduction of street railway fares. Some of them were manifestly unreasonable and would have undoubtedly reduced the profits of the company below ten per cent. Other proposed reductions have been considered without regard to their effect on the profits of the company, and under peculiar conditions the commission has ordered a reduction of fares; in such cases the company has complied without any complaint that the reduction would reduce its profits below ten per cent. on the cost of construction. The special committee on street railways advises that in place of the present limitation on the power of the board to reduce fares, it be provided that fares shall not be reduced by the commission below the average rate of fare charged for similar service by other street railways, which, in the judgment of the commission, are operated under substantially similar conditions.[1] Such a method of control appears to be based on the theory that the interests of the public and of the street railway companies are ordinarily identical, that therefore the average rate will be approximately the just rate, and that governmental interference is necessary only in certain exceptional cases.

be borne in mind however that probably a larger proportion of the street railways of Massachusetts are built along country highways, where the cost of construction is relatively light, than is the case in any other state.

[1] *Report of the Special Committee on Street Railways*, 1898, p. 53.

CHAPTER IX

GAS AND ELECTRIC LIGHT WORKS

1. *History of Development and Control*

ILLUMINATING gas was introduced in Massachusetts in 1823, with the incorporation of the Boston Gas Light Company by a special act of legislature.[1] The act provides that the company must obtain the written consent of the mayor and aldermen in order to dig up the streets for the laying and repairing of gas pipes, and to them is reserved the power to regulate the acts of the company that affect in any manner the health, safety, or convenience of the inhabitants of the city. The relation of gas companies to municipalities has continued practically on the basis here formulated down to within recent years.

It was not until about a quarter of a century after the incorporation of the Boston company that a general movement for the establishment of gas works in the other cities and towns of the state began. In 1855 the first general law for the incorporation of gas companies was passed.[2] It contains provisions almost identical with those already noted in the special act of 1823; and also the very important additional provision that in any city or town in which a gas company exists no similar company shall be incorporated unless the existing company has realized an annual dividend of seven per cent. on its capital stock for five years. By this provision any company that contented itself with a moderate

---

[1] Law of Jan. 22, 1823.   [2] *Acts*, 1855, 146.

return on its investment was guaranteed against competition. In 1870, however, this provision was repealed.[1]   Notwithstanding the existence of a general incorporation law, several companies have been incorporated by special act since 1855. But these special acts, as well as the special acts previous to 1855, contain provisions almost identical with those that have been noted in the first act of 1823, and which were afterwards included in the general law.

By an act of 1861 the governor and council were authorized to appoint an inspector of gas meters and illuminating gas.   It was made his duty to examine each meter intended for use, and to stamp and seal it if found to be correct. Upon request of the mayor and aldermen of a city or the selectmen of a town, it was his duty to test the gas supplied to the city or town to see that it was of the required legal standard.[2]   In 1880[3] the inspector was required to test the gas of every company supplying gas to fifty or more consumers at least twice a year.[4]

The marked success with which the railroad commission had dealt with the problem of railway regulation suggested the formation of a commission with similar powers for the regulation of gas companies.   Accordingly, a gas commission was established in 1885,[5] with most comprehensive powers of supervision, for the protection both of the companies and of the public.[6]   Previous to the establishment of the commission,

---

[1] Acts, 1870, 353.   [2] Ibid., 1861, 168.   [3] Ibid., 1880, 230.

[4] In 1866 the city of Boston made an extensive investigation concerning the manufacture and inspection of gas, and in the following year the mayor petitioned the legislature to grant the city a more extensive control over the gas companies, and also the right to appoint a city inspector of gas and gas-meters. But the legislature refused to grant the request. See Report on the Manufacture and Inspection of Gas, Boston Documents, 1866, no. 116; also House Documents, 1867, no. 469.

[5] Acts, 1855, 314.

[6] This was sixty-two years after the first company was incorporated, and about

aside from the very limited field of the state inspector, no attempt at administrative supervision had been made; no attempt had been made to secure publicity of accounts or to regulate rates; and no effective plan had been adopted to prevent over-capitalization. The municipality had no control over these matters, and the commonwealth had not seen fit to exercise the power that it possessed. The municipality, after permitting a company to lay mains in its streets, had a limited power to regulate its acts in the interest of the health, safety and convenience of its inhabitants, but this gave it no control over the rates, capitalization or accounts of the company. Nor were municipalities authorized to own and operate gas works.

The first electric light company was organized in 1880.[1] In six years the number had increased to forty. The companies were incorporated under a general law, and the cities and towns were required to grant the companies locations for their wires and poles, and had a limited power to regulate them.[2] As a result of this policy, within three years three cities had two companies each, and Boston had five. When the gas commission was established in 1885, electric light was just being introduced, and it was not deemed best to put it under the control of the commission at the time. But the development of electric light companies was so rapid and the connection between gas and electric light so intimate that two years later the commission was given the same power over electric light companies that it had in the case of gas companies.

Previous to 1891 municipalities had no authority to own

thirty-five years after the general movement had begun. Of the sixty-four gas companies existing in 1886, thirty-five were incorporated between 1850 and 1860, and all but thirteen were incorporated previous to 1870.—*Report of the Gas Commission*, 1886, p. 6.

[1] *Ibid.*   [2] *Acts*, 1883, 221.   [3] *Ibid.*, 1887, 382.

or operate gas or electric light works. In 1888, nevertheless, Danvers had erected an electric light plant for the
purpose of lighting its streets. The next year it petitioned
the legislature for permission to sell light and power, but
its petition was denied. Peabody attempted to establish a
plant but was restrained by the courts.[1]   At length in 1891,
on the petition of a number of cities and towns, the legislature passed a general law permitting municipalities to
purchase or erect gas and electric light plants for both
private and public lighting.[2]   Municipalities were required
first to purchase existing plants, and the municipal plants
were subjected to substantially the same supervision of the
gas and electric light commission as the private plants.

Thirteen towns and two cities now have their own gas or
electric light works. Two towns have plants for the supply
of both gas and electric light; the others supply only electric
light. In the short time that it has been permitted, municipal ownership has developed quite rapidly. One of the chief
difficulties in the way of municipal ownership is the fact that
the lighting business has to a considerable extent become
inter-municipal. In many cases it has been found most
economical to have but one plant for several municipalities.
In 1897 eighteen of the sixty-seven gas companies and
twenty-six of the eighty-three electric light companies were
supplying more than one city or town. The tendency has
been toward greater centralization. While this tendency
continues, the greater flexibility of private management is a
strong argument in its favor. We may rely upon private
corporations to consolidate whenever economy of operation
can be secured thereby, but we know that it is only very ex-

[1] Spaulding *v.* Peabody, 153 Mass., 129.

[2] *Acts,* 1891, 370. In the same year a special act was passed to legalize the
action of Danvers in establishing its plant.

traordinary conditions that will bring about the union of municipalities for the performance of a common function.

2. *The Gas and Electric Light Commission*

Since the establishment of the commission in 1885, its powers have been frequently amended, but always to increase and perfect them; the object being to place the commission in position to secure to the companies every opportunity for serving the public efficiently and economically, and to see that they make full use of their opportunities. As at present organized, the commission consists of three members appointed by the governor and council for terms of three years. The principle of partial renewal is adopted, the term of one member expiring annually. The members receive a salary and are not permitted to engage in any other business.[1] They can be removed only for cause, after notice and hearing.[2]

A most important power of the commission and the one on which the intelligent exercise of all others depends, is that of securing publicity. The commission prescribes the form and method of keeping accounts for both public and private works, and may inspect their accounts at any time. Since 1896, also, each company or municipality has been required to keep such records concerning the manufacture and distribution of gas or electric light as the commission may prescribe.[3] Annual reports must be made to the commission in the form and manner prescribed by it, and the manager of every municipal plant must in addition render a detailed report to the mayor or selectmen of the city or

[1] *Acts*, 1894, 503.

[2] The gas inspector still performs his duties independently of the commission, though required to furnish it information and assistance upon request.—*Acts*, 1885, 315.

[3] *Acts*, 1896, 356.

town, according to the form prescribed by the commission.
Gas and electric light companies are required to report to
the commission within twenty-four hours, all accidents caused
by gas or electricity,[1] and chiefs of police and medical examiners are required to report such accidents, whether occur-
ing in connection with municipal or private management.[2]
The facilities of the commission for getting at the facts necessary to hold the companies and the municipalities to a responsible performance of their public function, are therefore
almost complete ; all that is lacking is a periodical audit of
their accounts.

The commission has power on appeal to prevent municipalities from granting franchises to more than one gas or
electric light company.   In case a new company applies for
a franchise in a town already supplied by an existing company, the mayor and aldermen or the selectmen may, after
a public hearing, grant the request; an appeal may then be
taken to the commission, and its decision, made after giving
notice and hearing, is final.   In dealing with this problem,
the policy of the commission has been consistent.   It does
not consider competition possible or desirable in the lighting
business, and only in very exceptional cases will it permit a
duplication of plants.   This policy is well set forth in its
decision upon the appeal of the Worcester Electric Light Company :[3] "The history of corporations doing an electric lighting and similar business in competition in various parts of the
country affords strong ground for believing that a new company, if allowed to engage in business, would not long remain
by itself, as competition for a period would probably be followed, as elsewhere, by consolidation or absorption. Whether
or not such union would be for the public good, the com-

[1] *Acts*, 1888, 350.   [2] *Ibid.*, 1896, 338.
[3] *Report of the Gas and Electric Light Commission*, 1893, p. 24.

panies would see a gain thereby, and no power rests in this
Board or elsewhere, under existing laws, which could effectually prevent some form of consolidation.   If the advantages
incident to the growth of population, and the development
of business, are to be secured and retained for the benefit of
consumers, every reasonable effort must be made to prevent
unnecessary development of the capital chargeable upon the
business."   In conformity with this same policy, municipalities before undertaking municipal ownership, are required to
purchase existing plants.   As long as the companies properly perform their service to the community, they are free
from competition; they have a practical monopoly that is
abrogated only for cause. By this plan the risk to the investor
is greatly reduced, and he may very properly be called upon
to accept smaller dividends than would otherwise be
equitable.[1]

The commission has control over the consolidation of gas
companies with electric light companies; and it may after
notice and hearing authorize a gas company to furnish electric light.   But unless the gas company purchase the
franchise of an existing electric light company it must obtain
a franchise from the municipality in order to erect poles and
string wires.[2]   The policy of the commission has been to
favor consolidation in the smaller cities and towns, where by
that means economies in operation can usually be secured.
It argues that, " If a consolidation shall bring increased
strength and a larger measure of prosperity to the corporations, some share in these advantages will be received by the

---

[1] The question whether locations or franchises once granted may be revoked by
the municipality is not fully settled.   There is no statute specifically authorizing
either revocation or the exaction of compensation for the granting of locations;
either would be of very doubtful validity.   Legislation authorizing the exaction
of compensation has been frequently sought, but as yet has not been granted.

[2] *Acts*, 1887, 385.

community." But in the case of the gas and electric light companies of the city of Worcester[1] the commission refused to grant their petition to consolidate; holding that it would bring weakness rather than strength, and that consolidation would make it for their immediate interest to develop the sale of gas to the prejudice of electric light.[2]

In order to prevent overcapitalization, gas and electric light companies must secure the approval of the commission for each new issue of stock or bonds. New shares cannot be offered to stockholders at less than their market value, as determined by the commission.[3] Each year the commission is required to pass on numerous petitions of companies desiring to increase their capital stock, and each must be decided after a careful investigation of the peculiar conditions of the case. In deciding each case the two main points considered by the commission are (1) the purpose for which the new securities are to be issued, and (2) the relation of the present capitalization to a fair structural valuation of the plant. On the one hand an energetic development of the business must not be checked; and on the other, repairs that should be paid from income ought not to be made by an increase of capital, nor should earnings be capitalized that ought either to be spent in extending the business or in lowering the price to the consumer. If the commission finds the fair structural value of the plant to be less than the capitalization of the company, before allowing an issue of new stock or bonds it may prescribe such conditions and requirements as it deems best adapted to repair the capital stock within a reasonable time, or it may require the capital stock to be reduced by a prescribed amount.[4]

---

[1] Worcester then had a population of 84,655.

[2] *Report of the Gas and Electric Light Commission*, 1890, pp. 12–17.

[3] *Acts*, 1894, 450, 472.   [4] *Ibid.*, 1896, 473.

A gas or electric light company having a virtual monopoly of supplying a public service cannot be permitted to deny that service to any one who may be reasonably entitled to it. The commission may, therefore, after a public hearing, compel a company to furnish gas or electric light to any individual.[1]   In this matter also, it has the same power over municipalities that it has over companies.[2]

Upon complaint of the mayor or selectmen, or of twenty customers of any company, concerning the price or quality of the gas or electric light furnished, the commission after a public hearing may order the price reduced or the quality improved.   Municipalities cannot charge more for gas or electric light than will allow eight per cent. on the net investment, and they cannot charge less than actual cost except by written consent of the commission.   Each year the commission is compelled to pass on numerous petitions for cheaper or better light.   Many complaints are satisfactorily settled without any formal action on the part on the commission.   Since the formation of the commission, upon an average sixteen companies have annually reduced the price of gas.   Most of these reductions have come through the voluntary action of the companies.   They have been due largely to the competition caused by the increased activity and energy manifested in everything connected with lighting, and especially to the competition of electric lights.   They have been due also to the fact that the business, formerly largely speculative, has been placed on a substantial commercial basis; and with this the natural tendency has been to prefer a moderate rate of profit on a large investment rather than a large rate of profit on a small investment.   To bring about this condition has been one of the chief functions of the commission.   The average price of coal gas to the con-

---

[1] *Acts*, 1886, 346.   [2] *Ibid.*, 1891, 370.

sumer in 1886, the year after the creation of the commission, was $1.72 per thousand feet, in 1896 it was $1.17.[1]

It is the duty of the commission to see that all the provisions of law relative to companies or municipalities engaged in the sale of gas or electric light are observed; and it may apply to the attorney-general and the courts to enforce all such provisions and all lawful orders that it makes.[2]

State control over gas and electric light companies has certainly proved very efficient; whether municipal control might not be even better is, however, a very proper question. One difficulty in the way of municipal control, as in the case of municipal ownership, is that many of the plants supply several cities or towns. Here the lighting business has become an inter-municipal institution. It is possible, of course, to unite the towns served by a single company into a district for the purpose of exercising control over the company. Similar districts already exist for various purposes of administration. It is doubtful, however, whether the multiplication of local divisions is conducive to the highest political responsibility and efficiency.

There are, moreover, certain manifest advantages of control through a state commission. Efficient control must be of a quasi-judicial character, and must be exercised by men having an extensive technical knowledge of the subject. It does not seem probable that either of these essentials can be best secured through a local board. The state commission-

---

[1] *Report of the Gas and Electric Light Commission*, 1897, p. 108. The continuous decline in the price of gas is shown in the following table:

	1886	1887	1888	1889	1890	1891	1892	1893	1894	1895	1896
Average price of coal gas per m.	$1.72	$1.66	$1.56	$1.50	$1.46	$1.43	$1.52	$1.45	$1.26	$1.21	$1.17

[2] *Acts*, 1896, 426.

ers are paid good salaries, and devote all their time to the work. They thus gain greater experience and a better insight into the intricacies of the problem, than can possibly be gained by poorly paid, occasionally employed local boards. The public interest is best subserved by making the investment as secure as possible. If this is done the company can dispose of its bonds at a lower rate of interest, investors in its stock will be satisfied with smaller dividends, the business will be placed on a sure commercial basis, and the public will secure cheaper or better service. Investors can hardly fail to feel greater security if their interests are to be placed under the control of a state commission whose policy is well known, than under that of a local board whose policy can only be conjectured and is likely to be capricious. This being the case, municipalities, if permitted to choose in the matter, would probably find it to their interest to have the state commission perform this service for them. Municipalities might, with certain limitations, be permitted themselves to exercise control over the companies or to delegate that power to the state commission. There would then be a competition between the two methods of control, and with free competition the fittest may be trusted to survive.

CHAPTER X

THE CIVIL SERVICE COMMISSION

DOWN at least to the beginning of the present century the minister was the only professionally trained official in the service of the town. It is only recently that school teachers even have possessed special training. Popular administration has always been the rule. The plan adopted has in general been one of a great multiplicity of offices, simple duties, short terms, and compulsory, unpaid service. The theory is that each voter shall aid in administering the affairs of the town in accordance with his ability; and in order that he may do so without interfering seriously with his private affairs, the work is divided among a great number of persons. There is the least possible distinction between the governors and the governed. The policy decided upon in town meeting is popularly administered without the intervention of an official class.

But popular administration, in this sense of the term, is only possible under simple, primitive conditions. When the simple village community becomes a complex city, the complexity of the governmental organization must increase with the complexity of the conditions that it is its function to regulate. There must then be a division of labor. A comparatively small number of people must devote their entire time to the management of city business, while the great majority must devote themselves almost exclusively to private pursuits. The welfare of the community requires that both city and private business be conducted in the most economical and efficient manner, and both of these ends are furthered by a division of labor.   Moreover the complexity of city business requires the services of specially trained men.   The large city of the present requires the best skill of the lawyer, the teacher, the physician, the chemist, of the civil, the electrical and the mechanical engineer, and of men of almost every pursuit.

Under the former system each officer received his authority from the people of the town and was responsible to them. This system was followed by one of party administration and party responsibility.   Under this system each officer is responsible to his party and the party is responsible to the people.   The theory underlying this system has recently received its most vigorous expression from the mayor-elect of a great city.   He is reported to have said:

"The man for office under me must be honest, worthy, fit, yes; but he must be a Democrat, and the record of that man's Democracy must be pure and must be straight.   That is my notion of city government, and by that idea I will guide.   I do not do this on any 'To the victor belongs the spoils of the enemy' sentiment.   It is not a question of victory or of spoils.   The sole proposal is good government according to the expressed will of the people.   These latter have declared for the Democracy, they have elected its candidates and accepted its platform of principles.   With those as the conditions, what fashion of political man should be named to carry out those principles and keep the promises of that platform?   Should he be a Republican?   Or should he be a Democrat, who aided to make the platform; who believes in the principles set forth; who has fought for their success, and who has a heart to carry them into expression?   There can be only one answer to all this.   My appointees will be Democrats; none but Democrats."

This plan however has produced inefficiency in national,

commonwealth and municipal administration. Rotation in office, which is its natural result, is fatal to efficiency in most branches of the public service. The trouble arises from a failure to distinguish between the machine and the directing intelligence behind it. The administrative machine, if properly constituted, is as well adapted to the carrying out of a Republican as of a Democratic policy. Providing only the hand that directs it is in sympathy with the policy to be pursued, the administrative machine is as efficient in the administration of a high tariff as of a low tariff, of high license as of low license. This fact would doubtless be very generally recognized were it not for the supposed necessity of using the patronage to build up the party organization; of making the administrative machine serve also as the party machine. The strong temptation, therefore, to use the power of appointment and removal for partisan purposes has led to the necessity of placing that power under certain restrictions. The merit system has been the result.

The state civil service commission was established in 1884,[1] by " an act to improve the civil service of the commonwealth and the cities thereof." The commission is made up of three members, appointed and removable by the governor with the consent of the council. Not more than two of the commissioners can be of the same political party, and one commissioner retires every year. It appoints a chief examiner, a secretary, a registrar of labor, and the necessary clerks. For the local administration of the law, the commission appoints a board of examiners for each city. Appeals from the action of these local boards are heard by the state commission; and the members are removable at its pleasure.

At present, with certain express exceptions, the authority

---

[1] *Acts*, 1884, 320.

of the commission extends to all officers and employees of the commonwealth and of the cities, and of all towns of over twelve thousand inhabitants adopting the act. The following officers and employees are exempt by law from the civil service rules:[1] (1) judicial officers; (2) officers elected by the people, a city council, or either branch of the legislature; (3) officers whose appointment is subject to confirmation by the executive council of the commonwealth or by a city council; (4) the heads of the principal departments; (5) teachers in the public schools; (6) the employees of the commissioners of savings banks and of the treasurer and collector of taxes of cities and towns; (7) two employees of each city clerk, and the secretaries and confidential stenographers of the governor and of the mayors; (8) laborers in cities of less than one hundred thousand inhabitants, unless with the approval of the city council and mayor of the city.[2]

All other officers and employees may be brought under the rules of the commission. These rules may be general or special in their application. Among other things they must provide: (1) for a classification of the positions to be filled; (2) for the filling of vacancies in offices in accordance with the results of competitive or non-competitive examinations; (3) for the appointment of laborers in accordance with the results of examinations or otherwise; (4) for promotions in office on the basis of ascertained merit, seniority of service, or examination; (5) for a period of probation before an appointment is made permanent; and (6) for the preference of veterans in the certification of appointments, and for their certification without examination at the request of the appointing officer.[3]

The discretionary power thus vested in the commission is very great indeed. The law itself gives but little indication

---

[1] *Acts*, 1896, 502.   [2] *Ibid.*, 1896, 449.   [3] *Ibid.*, 1884, 320; *Ibid.*, 1896, 517.

of the actual extent to which the merit system has been applied or the actual methods adopted. For this one must look to the rules that have been adopted by the commission from time to time, with the approval of the governor and council.

The examinations held by the commission are both competitive and non-competitive. Non-competitive examinations may be provided in case of promotions, of temporary appointments, of positions for which there are no suitable candidates on the eligible list, and of positions requiring special information or skill. The eligible list is made up of those who have passed a competitive examination. Upon the requisition of the appointing officer the commission certifies the three names standing highest on the list; unless there are veterans on the list, in which case the law requires that they must be first certified without regard to rank.[1] Upon the request of the appointing officer, moreover, any veteran who has gone through the form of registering with the commission will be certified for appointment without examination. Any one of the three names certified may be selected. If no one of these persons is satisfactory, the commission, stating its reason therefor, may issue additional names. Within these limitations the responsibility for the appointment remains with the appointing officer, and, except in the case of veterans, the power to remove or reduce is not impaired. The veterans' preference law provides that no veteran in the service of any city or town shall be removed, suspended or transferred without a hearing before the mayor or selectmen.[2]

From the start the commission has adopted a conservative

[1] But if the appointing officer states in his requisition that he desires women, the veterans' preference does not apply.

[2] *Acts*, 1896, 517. See also the *Civil Service Rules* in the report of the commission for 1897.

policy; not attempting to make full use of the broad powers granted it. In its first report, the commission states that it has not attempted at once to apply the rules to all the positions included within the law, and that " only those branches of the service in which a considerable number of persons are employed, requiring qualifications which can be ascertained by simple and uniform tests, have been included in the present classification." This first classification included only the clerical, prison and police service of the commonwealth and the cities, and the fire and labor service of Boston—about 4,200 positions in all. In the following year the rules were extended to include draw-tenders of bridges and foremen of laborers in Boston. In 1887 this provision was made to apply to all cities, and the inspection service of all cities was also included. In its second report, the commission states that it has received applications from several cities, " requesting that the rules be extended to cover more of the subordinate officers and employees, especially the members of the fire departments and the laborers." The commission not having sufficient funds to make the extension requested, and the cities having no authority to make appropriations for such a purpose, the commission recommended that cities be given this power, arguing that " it would not only afford the several cities a local option of how far the system should be extended in their municipal affairs, but it would invite and encourage local interest and activity in the determination of this question, and would enable these communities to test more thoroughly the value of the system by its operation on a larger scale."

Accordingly in 1887 cities were granted authority to make appropriations to defray the expense of administering civil service rules.[1] In the following year the city of Cambridge

---

[1] *Acts*, 1887, 345.

requested that the rules be extended to its labor service, and made the necessary appropriation for that purpose. In the same voluntary manner New Bedford secured the application of the rules to its labor service in 1891, Newton in 1894, Everett in 1896, and Worcester in 1897. The policy of the commission has therefore been to make the application and continuance of the labor service rules optional except in the case of the city of Boston. This policy was to a certain extent fixed by law in 1896, by the adoption of an amendment to the law of 1888, providing that its provision in regard to the labor service shall not take effect in any city of less than one hundred thousand inhabitants except on its acceptance by the mayor and city council.[1]

In 1892, Cambridge again took the lead by officially requesting that the rules be extended to its fire service. The commission accordingly adopted a rule providing that the fire service of any city would be included in the classified service on the application of its mayor and aldermen. In the following year Somerville took advantage of this provision; New Bedford and Lowell followed in 1897. Owing to several accidents in the handling of steam by some of the school janitors of Boston, the school committee of that city petitioned the legislature for an act compelling the commission to include all the school engineers and janitors of the city in the classified service. This was done by the law of 1889.[2] Upon the request of Cambridge that its school janitors should also be included in the classified service, the commission adopted the rule that the school engineers and janitors of any city would be included at the request of the school committee of the city. Again on the petition of

---

[1] *Acts*, 1896, 449. In 1895, Boston was the only city of more than one hundred thousand inhabitants. Worcester had 98,767, and Fall River, 89,203.

[2] *Acts*, 1889, 352. *Report of the Civil Service Commission*, 1889, p. 8.

the school committee of Boston, all the truant officers appointed by it were by law included in the classified service.[1]

In 1894 an act was passed providing that any town of more than twelve thousand inhabitants might by vote bring itself under the provisions of the civil service law. Brookline, the only town of more than twelve thousand, took advantage of the provisions of the law during the same year.[2] A law of the same year provides for the appointment of inspectors of plumbing in every city and town having five thousand inhabitants or having a system of water supply or sewerage; and all inspectors before appointment are to be subjected to an examination by the commission.[3] In 1896 the commission made a further extension of its rules so as to include in the classified service the aids of the state fire marshal, and, of the city service, all messengers, all superintendents not exempted by statute, and all civil engineers, draughtsmen and other of the employees of the city engineer.[4]

In the gradual extension of the merit system through the voluntary action of the cities, the growing popularity of the system is clearly shown. We have noted how time after time the classified service has been extended by the civil service commission at the request of the cities concerned; this, in fact, has been the prevailing method by which extensions have been made. The question, therefore, naturally arises as to whether the adoption of the merit system might not better be left entirely to the option of the cities and towns. Although the development would have at first been slower, it seems probable that under a local option system most of the cities would have voluntarily placed their civil service under the rules of the state civil service commission.

[1] *Acts*, 1893, 253. *Report of the Civil Service Commission*, 1893, p. 8.

[2] *Acts*, 1894, 267. *Report of the Civil Service Commission*, 1894, p. 10.

[3] *Acts*, 1894, 455. *Report of the Civil Service Commission*, 1894, p. 9.

[4] *Report of the Civil Service Commission*, 1896, p. 8.

Yet it is also probable that were each city, desiring to adopt the merit system, required itself to administer the system, instead of leaving its administration as at present to a state civil service commission, very few cities would undertake the reform. It can hardly be expected that a small city with but a small number of persons in its service, will go to the trouble and expense of establishing the machinery necessary for the independent administration of the merit system.

Centralized administration seems in this case to be the most economical, efficient and reliable. It is more economical because a separate commission for each city would lead to the needless repetition of work now performed but once for all by the central commission. It is more efficient because ordinarily the state commission would be composed of members of a higher grade than those of the local commissions. It is more reliable because entirely independent of the local administration and therefore not open to the suspicion of being influenced by it. The function of the commonwealth seems here to be properly, not regulation or compulsion, but the tender of its services through the civil service commission to those cities that desire to secure the benefits of the merit system. We would then have central administration for the purpose of serving the localities rather than for the exercise of control over them.

The merit system was instituted for the purpose of doing away with the spoils system, but in its actual application it does more than this: it has enormously increased the competition for office both in quantity and quality. Without the merit system, the appointing power is practically limited in selecting his subordinates to his personal acquaintances or persons recommended by them. Having no means of testing the actual ability of the applicant, the appointing officer, if possible, selects a person concerning whom he has some personal knowledge—preferably a relative or friend. With the adoption of the merit system, all may enter the competition on equal terms. It secures equality of opportunity, and this results in the placing of the round pegs in the round holes.

CHAPTER XI

CENTRAL AUDIT, LOCAL RECORDS, STATE HIGHWAYS AND THE METROPOLITAN DISTRICT

1. *The Audit of County Accounts*

THE county has never been a vigorous institution in Massachusetts. It is little more than an administrative district for purposes of state administration. Its chief function is the maintenance of courts and prisons. Until 1855 county officers were appointed by the governor and council, and judges, justices and medical examiners are still so appointed. When the counties were first established their boundaries were doubtless determined with reference to convenience as administrative districts; but population has moved and the boundaries have remained fixed until now they are not at all adapted to the purposes for which they exist. Norfolk county is composed of three separate parts: two of its towns are inside of neighboring counties. It is not to be expected, therefore, that any vigorous local interest will be taken in county administration; its efficiency must largely depend upon state supervision.

In 1874 the house committee on finance, after investigating the accounts of county officers, reported that it was impossible to conceive " of a more loose, irresponsible and grossly defective method of transacting public business." [1] A special committee was charged with the further investigation of the matter, and its report of the following year shows that the evils had not been exaggerated. It reports " that more than

---

[1] *House Documents*, no. 493, 1874.

half the justices appear to have performed their administrative duties as suited their own notions and convenience, without the slightest regard for the requirements of law." In Barnstable county the treasurers were accustomed to retain their books and accounts upon leaving the office. In Franklin county the treasurer never balanced his accounts. "Some treasurers balance their accounts monthly; others yearly. We think a private corporation would hardly allow a bookkeeper to run his cash account a week without making a balance." [1]

No action was taken until four years later. In 1879 the commissioners of savings banks were given supervision over the accounts of a large number of county officers. [2] They were required to inspect personally, at least once a year, the books and accounts of county treasurers, commissioners, sheriffs, jailers, masters of houses of correction, district attorneys, clerks of courts, bail commissioners, registers of probate and insolvency, and registers of deeds. They were authorized to require uniformity in methods of keeping accounts. Each of these officers was required to make an annual report of receipts and expenditures to the bank commissioners in the manner prescribed by them.

The bank commissioners continued to audit county accounts until 1887. Though they accomplished much, their work was not as thorough or satisfactory as it might have been, or as they themselves desired. A multiplicity of other duties prevented them from devoting sufficient time to the work. Furthermore, police courts and trial justices were omitted from their supervision, and as these officers turned over large sums of money to the county treasurer, the commissioners could not ascertain accurately the correctness

[1] *House Documents*, no. 18, 1875.

[2] *Acts*, 1879, 293; *Acts*, 1880, 161.

of the accounts of that officer. At the suggestion of the commissioners they were relieved of their control over county accounts, and the office of controller of county accounts was created.[1]

The controller of county accounts is appointed and removable by the governor and council. His powers differ from those of the bank commissioners chiefly in that Suffolk county is exempt from his supervision, and the inferior courts and trial justices have been brought under his control.[2] The county treasurer and all the officers that are required to pay money to him are under the supervision of the controller. He is also required to examine the official bonds of county officers,[3] and to audit and certify the monthly traveling expenses of county commissioners.[4]

It has long been the custom of the legislature annually to vote the appropriations and the tax levy for each county except Suffolk. This is largely a mere matter of form; its chief merit lies in the publicity that it involves rather than in the exercise of a wise discretion on the part of the legislature. County commissioners are required to submit annual estimates of receipts and expenditures to the state controller in the form prescribed by him. It is then the duty of the controller to analyze and classify these estimates, as nearly as possible on a uniform basis, and report them to the legislature; and he is required to send a copy of this report to the mayor or selectmen of each city and town.[5]

The work of the controller in examining and supervising county accounts has proved most valuable. The irresponsible methods shown in the investigations of 1874 and 1875 have

---

[1] *Acts*, 1887, 438.

[2] The affairs of Suffolk county are attended to by the city of Boston. The city auditor exercises the supervision ·that in the other counties is exercised by the state controller.

[3] *Acts*, 1890, 380.   [4] *Ibid.*, 1893, 273.   [5] *Ibid.*, 1895, 143; *Ibid.*, 1897, 153.

been corrected. The light which the controller has thrown upon the hitherto obscure and devious methods of county administration has led to several important reforms. The publicity which his work has secured has enabled the people to exercise a more effective control over the officers elected by them than was formerly possible. It is perhaps needless to argue that this work could not be as efficiently performed by a local officer. From the greater experience gained by devoting all his time to the auditing of county accounts the state officer is able to render better service; he is an expert. The work of a local auditor is always open to the suspicion of being affected by personal or local influences. State audit has the essential element of reliability.

In the future we may expect a demand to arise for the extension of this service to the cities and towns. It is a service which, under even the most favorable local conditions, can best be rendered by the central government.

2. *The Commissioner of Public Records*

The very unsatisfactory condition of the public records in the towns and counties led to the appointment of a special commissioner to investigate the subject in 1884.[1] The commissioner made his report in 1889.[2] He found the records to be very incomplete, and in many cases existing records were in the hands of private individuals instead of the officials designated by law. Few towns had any safe place for keeping their records. The commissioner thought that there was ample legislation on the subject if it could only be enforced, and recommended that the existing commission be continued for a sufficient length of time to enable it to bring all the records available into the custody of the officers designated by law. He says: "I would not recommend

[1] *Resolves*, 1884, c. 65.
[2] *Report on the Public Records of Parishes, Towns and Counties.*

the creation of a record commission, to be erected on the model of the English Record Commission, for it seems to me wise to preserve and stimulate local interest in records. If they were to be brought to a central office, this interest would decline."

The special commission was continued for three years, and then in 1892 the office of commissioner of public records was established. It is the duty of this officer "to take such action as may be necessary to put the public records of the counties, cities, towns, churches, parishes or religious societies of the commonwealth in the custody and condition contemplated by the various laws relating to such records, and to secure their preservation." [1]

Through the influence of the record commissioner vaults and safes have been provided until almost every city and town has its most important records fairly secure. Many important records have been printed and copies of others have been made. Nevertheless the records of many of the towns are far from being in the condition contemplated by the statutes and are very inconvenient for purposes of consultation. The record commissioner and many historical workers are therefore of the opinion that the English system should be adopted, that all parish and town records prior to a date to be fixed upon should be brought to a central office of fireproof construction, and there classified and indexed and put in a proper condition for preservation.

3. *The Highway Commission*

During the last decade of the eighteenth and the first few decades of the nineteenth century, there was considerable activity in road building. Numerous turnpike corporations were formed and extensive turnpikes were constructed. With the building of railroads, however, the care of the high-

[1] *Acts*, 1892, 333.

way was lost sight of.　It is only with the practical completion of the railway system that attention has again been
turned to the improvement of the highway.　Formerly the
highway was the medium not only of local, but also of
through transportation.　Although now reduced to a subordinate position, it is as indispensable as ever.　Good roads
are necessary in order to secure the maximum of advantage
from the railway; they form an indispensable part of any
complete system of transportation.

In the present movement for good roads the bicycle has
been the important factor.　The farmer was satisfied to use
the roads that he had always used.　It was the wheelmen
who first appreciated the value of a level track.　Chiefly as
the result of an agitation carried on by them, a special commission was appointed in 1892 to report upon a plan for the
construction of state highways.　In accordance with the
plans recommended by it, a permanent state highway commission was established in the following year.[1]　The commission consists of three members appointed by the governor
and council for terms of three years.　They may be removed
by the governor with the consent of the council for such
stated cause as he may deem sufficient.

It is the duty of the commission to compile statistics and
carry on investigations concerning the roads of the state, and
to collect information concerning the best materials for road
building.　The commission may be consulted without charge
by all local authorities concerning the construction and
maintenance of roads; and it is required to hold annually at
least one meeting in each county for the discussion of road
improvement.

Upon petition of the mayor and aldermen of a city, the
selectmen of a town, or the county commissioners of a

[1] *Acts*, 1893, 476.

county, the highway commission may accept a road as a state highway, to be constructed and maintained by the commission at the expense of the commonwealth. The commission may contract for the construction of the road either with the city or town in which the road is situated or with private parties. One-quarter of the cost of construction must be repaid to the commonwealth by the county within six years. The commission may also contract with the city or town, or with private parties, for the maintenance of the highway, and it cannot be dug up or altered in any way without a permit from the commission. The construction of state roads must be apportioned fairly between the different counties, and not more than ten miles can be constructed in any county during any one year without the approval of the governor and council.[1]

During the four years 1894–97, 1,094.4 miles of road were petitioned for and 179.2 miles laid out. The road laid out is situated in 121 different cities and towns.[2] While at present these little strips of road are widely scattered and disconnected, it is the purpose of the commission that they shall eventually form parts of an extensive and well-planned system. The commission has in view the connection of centers of business with each other. In case there is a large traffic between two cities or towns by way of a road passing through other towns which profit little by the traffic, the road is to be taken as a state road. The commission also has in view the connection of the large centers of population with the surrounding agricultural areas. Each large city is to have roads radiating from it in all directions. Moreover the now declining towns remote from the railroads and waterways, are to be taken from their isolation and con-

[1] *Acts*, 1894, 497.

[2] *Report of the Massachusetts Highway Commission*, 1897, pp. 145-6.

nected with the business centers.   Finally there are to be a
number of continuous highways throughout the commonwealth.[1]

4. *The Metropolitan District*

The area known as the metropolitan district consists of
the territory lying within about ten miles of the city hall of
Boston; it includes Boston and its suburbs.   The history of
this area shows first a period of division and then one
of consolidation.   In 1640 there were ten towns wholly or
partly within this area.   By 1860, through the process of
settlement and division already described, the number had
been more than trebled.

Now, however, forces tending toward consolidation and
centralization came into play.   The immense population
which the centralization of industry had massed in Boston
began to overflow into the adjoining towns.   This movement was greatly accelerated by the development of the
horse railway.   Gradually in this way Boston and a number
of its adjoining towns were merged in everything but name
and government into a single community.   As a result some
of these towns were at length annexed to Boston; Roxbury
in 1867, Dorchester in 1869, and Charlestown, Brighton and
West Roxbury in 1873.[2]   Brookline, which until 1705 was a
part of Boston, was by these annexations almost surrounded
by the territory of that city, but in spite of this fact it has
retained an independent municipal existence down to the
present time.

Though there have been no further annexations to Boston,
the forces which led to them have continued unabated.
The spreading out of population has been given an enormous

---

[1] *Report of the Massachusetts Highway Commission*, 1897, pp. 15–19.

[2] During this period also two new towns were formed from the division of existing towns; Hyde Park in 1868 and Everett in 1870.

impetus by the development of electric lines since 1889. They have made land formerly of use only for agriculture available for residence purposes. They have organized the entire district consisting of twenty-nine cities and towns into a single community with a common center.

As early as 1872 the common needs of the district led to an attempt to have a special commission appointed to report a plan for a system of sewerage and water supply. The state board of health says in regard to this, "It seems to us of great importance in the interest of public health that some comprehensive system be adopted."[1]   A special metropolitan drainage commission was authorized by the legislature in 1881.   In its report it recommended the establishment of a drainage district to consist of Boston and twenty other cities and towns. Another special commission reported on the same subject in 1885, but its labors, too, were without immediate results. Finally, in 1889, the state board of health reported plans for a sewerage system for the Mystic and Charles river valleys, and a board of metropolitan sewerage commissioners was established to carry out these plans. The board consists of three salaried members appointed by the governor, with the consent of the council, for terms of three years.   The method of partial renewal is adopted: the term of one member expiring annually.   It is its duty to build, maintain and operate a system of main sewers for Boston and seventeen other cities and towns, situated in the Mystic and Charles river valleys.[2]   In 1895 it was authorized to provide a similar system for the cities and towns of the Neponset river valley, consisting of Boston, Dedham, Hyde Park and Milton.[3]

In 1892 a special commission was appointed to " consider the advisability of laying out ample open spaces for the use

---

[1] *Report of the State Board of Health*, 1872, p. 7.

[2] *Acts*, 1889, 439,   [3] *Ibid.*, 1895, 406.

of the public, in the towns and cities in the vicinity of Boston."[1] In accordance with its recommendations a board of metropolitan park commissioners was established with broad powers to establish and maintain an extensive system of parks and boulevards for a district including twelve cities and twenty-five towns.[2] The commission consists of five unsalaried members appointed by the governor and council for terms of five years. The term of one member expires annually, and they are subject to removal by the governor.

Upon the recommendation of the state board of health a metropolitan water board was created in 1895.[3] It consists of three salaried members appointed and removable by the governor and council. Their term of office is three years, one member retiring annually. At least one of the three must be a resident of Boston and one a resident of the district outside of Boston. It is the duty of the board to construct, maintain and operate substantially in accordance with the plans prepared by the state board of health, a system of water supply for a metropolitan district, including seven cities and six towns, and all other cities and towns within ten miles of the state house requesting to be admitted to the district.

The work of these metropolitan commissions has been very satisfactory. Nevertheless it is felt that they are merely a temporary expedient; that sooner or later some plan will be adopted to provide for the common needs of the district through officers directly responsible to it. If at the time these commissions were formed this district had been included within the bounds of a single county, the task of providing for these common needs would doubtless have de-

---

[1] *Acts*, 1892, 342.   [2] *Ibid.*, 1893, 407; *Ibid.*, 1894, 288; *Ibid.*, 1895, 450.

[3] *Ibid.*, 1895, 488.

volved upon the county authorities; but the county, as at present constituted, has become a well-nigh useless institution in Massachusetts. County lines as originally established were determined with reference to the common needs to be served; but conditions have changed and the lines have remained fixed, and now the metropolitan district includes one entire county and parts of three others. Territorial lines should neither divide people with like interests nor unite people with unlike interests; the problem is so to adjust the territorial boundary as to include a maximum of like with a minimum of unlike interests. In order that this may be brought about frequent readjustment is necessary. But it is here that the rigidity of governmental organization is most pronounced. Failure to make these readjustments is usually excused in the interest of the preservation of historical associations, but historical associations of the highest value center about the common life of the community rather than about any definite territorial area; they demand that boundary lines shall express the common life rather than cramp or divide it.

The demand for some form of local government for the metropolitan district led to the appointment of a special commission to consider the subject in 1894.[1] This commission made its report in 1896. It does not favor the formation of a consolidated city by the annexation of all the suburban cities and towns to Boston. It recommends that, while preserving local initiative and local autonomy in all matters where the service can be undertaken and carried on by the respective cities and towns working within their own borders, a county with a county council at its head should be established for the execution of larger and more general undertakings. The district which it proposes to include in

---

[1] *Acts*, 1894, 446.

this county contains twenty-nine cities and towns; it has an area of 273.07 square miles, and in 1895 contained a population of 982,037, of whom 494,205 were residents of Boston.[1]

While the county system of organization is for the present at least doubtless the best, there is need for the consolidation of many of the petty municipalities into which the district is divided. The average area of these cities and towns, excluding Boston, is 8.2 square miles, and they vary in population from 864 to 81,519. As long as a municipality has a distinct common life, consolidation is premature; but when, as is in many cases a fact, the boundary line between two municipalities is no more distinct than the boundaries of an election district in an ordinary city, continued separation is a disorganizing element. The tendency of a wider social and industrial organization is more and more to merge these once distinct communities into a common whole. But while social and industrial relations have become organized on a wider basis, it is still attempted to organize government on a neighborhood basis. Under modern city conditions a man's real neighbors are not the people who happen to live in the same district or building that he does, but those whom he meets in the work-shop, the store, the labor union, the social club and the church. With the progress of civilization, association depends less and less on mere physical contiguity and more and more upon an identity of economic, social and intellectual interests.

[1] See *Report of the Metropolitan District Commission*, 1896.

CHAPTER XII

THEORY OF THE RELATION OF COMMONWEALTH TO
MUNICIPAL ACTIVITY.

THE relation of the municipality to the commonwealth is
not simply that of a subordinate to a superior. It is a relation of a much higher and more complex character. Each
has a distinct sphere of activity and a distinct individuality.
Each has rights to be respected by the other, and duties in
the interest of the other; each is an organ of the state.

This follows from a consideration of the position of the
municipality and the commonwealth in the economic organization of society. Upon the economic organization of
society depend the territorial distribution and grouping of
population. These groups or communities are of all sizes;
the smaller being included within the larger, and these within
still more extensive groups. The grouping of population
about a common center leads to the development of common needs that can best be met by collective effort. Each
such community will naturally provide institutions for the
satisfaction of these common needs. It is thus that the town
governments in Massachusetts were first formed. These
communities are not the creation of a central government,
they are the product of the existing economic organization;
and territorial divisions, in so far as they are what they
should be, will conform to them. Territorial boundaries
should not be arbitrary, but should express the common life
of the community.

Commonwealth lines in New England express past rather

than present conditions; they express the community of interest incident to a stage-coach regime rather than to one of the railroad and the telegraph. Had New England been settled under modern conditions as have the western commonwealths, it would have formed a single commonwealth instead of six. It would form a commonwealth of a little less than the average area and would rank third in population. New England has a marked individuality. The community of interest that really exists is evidenced by the very large number of New England organizations. Industry, and almost everything but government, is organized along New England rather than commonwealth lines.

The individuality of the cities and towns of Massachusetts is in most cases very marked. The political boundaries correspond in large measure to the natural boundaries. In the rural towns there is little demand for collective activity. In the cities, however, a vigorous community life is very evident. The city itself is clearly not the creature of the legislature, though under present conditions its government is. It is not an arbitrary territorial division, but a natural economic development. It is primarily a mobilization of labor and capital for greater division of labor and co-operation: it is also in itself a division of labor, being a product of the localization of industry. This implies a certain degree of individuality; but it is not individual in the sense of being self-sufficient or independent, but in the true sense of being a specialized organ for the performance of a special function. As such, like the individual, it should have all rights and immunities necessary for the full performance of its function, and all duties and limitations necessary to secure the rights and immunities of other organs.

The true relation of the municipality to the commonwealth is in many respects analogous to the relation of the individual to the commonwealth. In all civilized states the individual has a sphere of liberty or self-government, upon which government either does not or cannot encroach. The tendency in all states is to widen the sphere of individual immunity; the delimitation of a broad sphere of individual self-government has during the past century been one of the chief concerns of constitution-makers. The totality of the activities of the state have been more or less definitely divided between the individual and the government; both are organs through which the ends of the state are attained.[1]

One of the most important rights of the individual is his general right of independent initiative. His individuality is not repressed by his being limited to certain specific and enumerated activities. He has a general grant of power; he may undertake any activity which has not been expressly denied him or granted to some other authority. This is one reason why the individual is so versatile, so quick to undertake new enterprises; he does not have to wait for an act of the legislature.

The individual has been a brilliant success in America, while municipal government has been a comparative failure. This failure is probably largely due to the lack of a general grant of power on the part of the municipality. The city is naturally the pioneer in a broad field of undertakings. The greater centralization of wealth and population in the city creates new necessities and makes possible the provision of many new conveniences. The city is a leader in social organization. The improved methods which centralization permits it to originate are but slowly diffused through the rest of the community. Most of these new necessities and conveniences are supplied by private enterprise, but many require the direct or the indirect interference of the city government. In order that a continuous progress may not be

[1] See Burgess, *Political Science and Comparative Constitutional Law*, pp. 87–89.

prevented, it is, therefore, of the utmost importance that the city should be in position to respond at once to the new demands that are made upon it; it is essential that it should possess the power of initiation. This is far from being the case, however. The entire municipal organization is prescribed by statute in the greatest detail, and nothing can be done that is not specifically authorized. The needs of the municipality are constantly changing, but it cannot make any change in its organization or undertake any new activity without first receiving the express authorization of the legislature. The changes which should come about automatically with the changing needs of the community, are brought about, if at all, by the tardy and arbitrary methods of special legislation. This is at present the most demoralizing element in municipal government. In Germany and France the municipalities have a general grant of power;[1] and as we have already seen, this was the system under which the institutions of the Massachusetts town were first developed. It is to this system that the remarkable strength and vigor of those institutions can be largely attributed. A return to this system would introduce new life and vigor into municipal government.

Assuming then a municipality with a general grant of power, what is its natural sphere of activity? In the first place there is a division of functions between the individual and the government as a whole; then there is division of governmental functions between the national and the commonwealth governments. Assuming that these divisions have taken place, upon what principles does the further distribution of commonwealth functions between the central and the local governments depend?

First. Where government undertakes to exercise control

---

[1] Goodnow, *Municipal Problems*, p. 50.

over a given institution, the question of whether this control shall be administered centrally or locally will naturally turn upon the extent of the institution in question. For the exercise of efficient control, the jurisdiction of the controlling authority must be as extensive as the institution controlled. An officer whose jurisdiction covers but a single town cannot exercise efficient control over a railroad, telegraph or express company.[1]

Second. Whether certain functions shall be administered centrally or locally depends upon substantially the same factors that determine whether a given industry shall be centralized or decentralized. The economies of production on a large scale cause the large producer to crowd out the smaller. The benefits of increased specialization can be obtained only by a more comprehensive organization. This is as true in certain branches of public administration as it is in industry. Each town might maintain a separate prison, insane asylum, and university, but equal efficiency could be obtained under this system only at an expense that would render it practically out of the question. The needs of classification and specialization require organization on a more comprehensive basis.[2]

Third. It being determined that a certain function shall be administered in the localities, the question that then arises is whether it shall be administered independently by the local authorities, by the local authorities under a central supervision, or by centrally-appointed and responsible officials. The answer to this question depends, in the first place, upon whether the efficient performance of the function is a matter of local or general concern. If exclusively of local concern, there is of course no demand for central interference. If, on the other hand, it be a matter of general concern, there may

[1] See above pp. 71, 74, 79, 120.   [2] See above pp. 27, 37, 49, 62.

or may not be cause for central interference; this will depend upon whether there exists in the performance of the function an identity of interest between the municipality and the commonwealth.

If there is an identity of interest between the municipality and the commonwealth, there is no occasion for central interference; the general welfare will be cared for by the self interest of the municipality. Street cleaning and the maintenance of sewers and water supplies are, upon the whole, examples of this class of functions. If, however, the interests of the two are not in all respects identical, a certain degree of central supervision and control will be necessary. Poor relief is perhaps the best illustration of this.[1]

But, when in the performance of a given function, the interests of the municipality and the commonwealth are directly antagonistic, it is usually better for the commonwealth to perform the function through its own officers than to compel the municipality to act as its agent. Compulsory service, once the rule on the part of the individual, has been very generally discarded as inefficient. As applied to municipalities it is even more unsatisfactory. When the local sentiment is opposed to the enforcement of a law restraining the individual, it will usually take as great an expenditure of energy on the part of the central officials to secure even a tardy enforcement of the law by the local officials, as would be required should they take its enforcement into their own hands. This is usually true in the case of prohibitory liquor laws, and often in the case of compulsory school attendance laws. The recognition of the principle brought about the establishment and maintenance of a state police force in Massachusetts.[2]

Governmental functions having been distributed between

---

[1] See above pp. 38, 54, 73, 98.   [2] See above pp. 73, 79, 80, 85, 89, 93.

the municipality and the commonwealth according to the principles above indicated, what is the proper relation of the commonwealth to the municipality as such? The municipality, acting as the agent of the commonwealth in the administration of functions in which there is not a complete identity of interest between the municipality and the commonwealth, should, as we have seen, be subjected to supervision and control; but it is also necessary that the commonwealth should, to a certain extent, aid and regulate the municipality when acting in furtherance of purely local needs. Here the analogy of the relation of the individual to the commonwealth is very apparent. The commonwealth regulates the individual in his relations with other individuals, and assists him by performing for him certain services that he cannot, or cannot efficiently and economically, perform for himself. The commonwealth stands in a similar relation to the municipality. It must regulate, to a considerable extent, the relations of the municipality to the individual and to other municipalities. Control over municipal taxation and boundaries is illustrative of this field of regulation.[1] In the regulation of the municipality, however, there is no occasion for the close supervision that is maintained over the individual. There are municipalities that are occasional wrong-doers, but there is no class of criminally disposed municipalities, as there is of individuals. There may, however, be defective and dependent classes of municipalities that stand in need of special aid and supervision. Some of the small declining rural towns of Massachusetts may be

---

[1] At present the commonwealth exercises control over these matters, but the control exercised is legislative and not administrative. Legislative control is as inferior to administrative in these matters as it is in the case of *quasi*-public corporations. Similar benefits may be expected to accrue from the establishment of a board to exercise control over municipal taxation, loans, boundaries and other matters pertaining to the municipality as such, to those that have admittedly resulted from the establishment of a state board of railroad commissioners.

classed as dependents, and a few of its summer resort towns might possibly be classed as defectives.[1]   It is the province of the commonwealth moreover to assist the municipality as such, by performing for it certain services that it cannot, or cannot efficiently and economically, perform for itself. Of this nature are such services as the administration of the merit system, the technical regulation of municipal monopolies, the audit of municipal accounts, and generally the entire field of municipal inspection and the securing of the greatest possible publicity concerning municipal conditions.[2]

The relation between the municipality and the commonwealth is organic and not mechanical.   The problem is to recognize the individuality and responsibility of each.   There must be centralization without consolidation and fusion, decentralization without divorce and isolation.   There must be sufficient centralization to secure the autonomy of the commonwealth, .sufficient decentralization to secure the autonomy of the municipality, sufficient control to secure the responsibility of each.

[1] See above pp. 35, 48, 53.   [2] See above, pp. 136, 145, 151, 152.